NOW I KNOW I AM NOT ALONE

A true story of cancer, everyday miracles, and hope

FRANK DANZA

ISBN 978-1-64492-965-0 (paperback)
ISBN 978-1-64492-966-7 (digital)

Christian Faith Publishing, Inc.
832 Park Avenue
Meadville, PA 16335
www.christianfaithpublishing.com

Printed in the United States of America

To my scores of family and friends and the scores of their family and friends who prayed for me when I needed those prayers the most and for those who continue to pray for me today.

You asked, and He provided. Every second that we pray matters.

CONTENTS

FOREWORD

I recall first meeting Frank Danza and his wife, April, in July of 2000, only several short weeks into my pastorate at St. Mark's parish, Brooklyn, New York. At that time, it had been brought to my attention on various occasions that there was no signage anywhere around the large Church building indicating the name of the parish. I decided to publicize in the parish bulletin if there might be anyone interested in memorializing such a sign for our Church. The first weekend this request was published in the parish bulletin, both Frank and April made an appointment to see me and stated their desire to sponsor the sign. Our faith community had a name, St. Mark, and the public statement made by the presence of this sign, front and center, was a profound first step in what would become the revitalization of our faith community.

I share this story because it speaks to me regarding the premise of this book, namely to recognize and name, as the sign prominently standing outside the Church, the countless manifestations of God's love in our lives. What we can often perceive as haphazard isolated events are recognized by the author as one seamless journey of our unique individual lives. In describing the occurrences of our daily lives, coincidence is often simply perceived as chance or luck. Yet an appreciation of the miracles spoken of in this book by the author implies a belief in the deeper intelligence at work, namely God. Carl Jung, the psychologist, developed the concept *synchronicity* in describing two or more events that are causally unrelated yet are experienced as occurring together in a meaningful manner. This "meaningful manner" by which seemingly unrelated occurrences of our lives are joined is what is known to the Catholic Christian believer as the mystery of the Triune God.

How many times do we ask ourselves, what is that something present within all our lives that's difficult to understand and impossible to explain? As is spelled out in the pages of this book, that "mystery" is the presence of God we innately sense as so real yet seemingly always illusive.

A "Monday morning quarterback" looks back to analyze past isolated events in an attempt to effect change in the future. On the other hand, the person who embraces "the mystery" understands both yesterday and tomorrow not as fractionalized and disconnected but times of one continuous encounter with the living God, as lived out in the present moment. For Christ Himself is the Alpha and the Omega. All time belongs to Him.

And so, as we are helped to realize in this book, the occurrences in our lives remain unrelated, like individual letters of the alphabet, until the reality of God within allows us to recognize their connectedness, thus joining these "letters" into complete words that begin to make sense for us.

Rabbi David Zaslow writes that the Hebrew word *shalom* means something even greater than "peace." It speaks of a "wholeness" within ourselves. A belief that there is a connection to all our comings and goings. They are wondrously linked together.

I know *shalom* will truly be the gift to all who reflectively read this book: the story of one life now lived with a recognition of the great miracle of God, who makes all things new. From reading this book, I now live life with an even greater conviction that truly with God, all things become possible.

Reverend Monsignor Joseph R. Grimaldi, JCL, VE
Diocese of Brooklyn

Life's journey is never clear and direct. It can feel like a wandering path that is sometimes filled with wondrous and joyous moments and, at other times, tragic and devastating pitfalls. Out of those tragic events, sometimes an individual develops insights and revelations that can have a profound effect, changing us to the core, giving us an understanding of life that we never experienced.

Our author Frank Danza takes us on such a journey. He shares his life from his humble family upbringing to his ascent to one of the nation's foremost experts in the field of financial revenue cycle management. I have known Frank the businessman, the entrepreneur, the planner. But this book is not about the career of a man; it is far more personal. In this book, Frank shares with us his personal dreams, aspirations, and plans. But even that only sets the stage for how this intelligent, logical, fact-driven man comes to understand that not all we face can be explained.

This book is a touching story of a man's life. Frank allows us to understand how his values and beliefs were established early in life through his close-knit extended Italian family. He shares how he learned the value of hard work while working in the family business. He reveals his deep and strong religious beliefs that are reinforced through the love of his family. He shares the joys in his life, his wife, his children, and his amazing career. Frank also shares his most life-changing event: his fight with cancer.

Frank was diagnosed with advanced renal cell carcinoma. An event that truly changed his life—not for the fight that he endures battling this disease but for how this battle gave him new understandings on how we do not walk alone in this life. He believes that God, or however you define a higher power, watches over us, protects us, and helps us on our journey. Logic, facts, science cannot explain everything. There is so much we do not understand. When life leads us in an unusual direction, we write that off to chance or luck. Frank provides compelling evidence that in his life, there is no chance or coincidence—that everything happens for a reason, that you are in the time and place in your life exactly where and when you should be. He does not dismiss free will, yet Frank makes a compelling argument that every once in a while, God may "nudge" you to make a decision that you do not understand. Frank holds that these are life's little miracles, that these miracles happen all the time in everybody's lives; however, we are too busy to understand or realize they are happening. Through Frank's battle with his disease and his fortuitous connection with the Healer, Frank has come to realize that God had a plan for his life all along.

Inspiring, moving, and thought-provoking, Frank's story is a wonderful read. It helps you question what we take for granted every day. I thank Frank for the courage to share such a personal journey and for making us examine what small miracles have shaped our lives that we were simply too preoccupied to recognize.

Mark J. Solazzo
Executive Vice President and Chief Operating Officer
Northwell Health

PREFACE

I was visiting John one Wednesday evening. It was the fall of 2017. I was sitting in the armchair right next to his desk; he was seated in his desk chair, facing me with his hands extended over my chest. This was a typical scene whenever I visited John, and he and I had a standing appointment: Wednesday night at six thirty. Almost every Wednesday night.

We were about half the way through our session, and I was resting with my eyes closed. John broke the silence, "God wants me to show you how He works." I responded unemotionally, "Okay." He then walked in front of me, and we held hands. He began to pray. John closed his eyes, and with absolutely no expression on his face, he became completely quiet. He swayed ever so gently left to right and left again as we faced each other, holding hands. He was standing in front of me while I sat in the same chair I sat in during every visit. What happened next is the most incredible and special thing that has ever happened to me, something I have recalled joyfully every single day since and I am sure I will continue to recall every day for the rest of my life.

John's face began to change. His cheekbones became higher, and his cheeks became narrowed. His narrowed cheeks came to a small point under his mouth, forming a new chin where a small rounded chin used to exist. His mouth became smaller, and his pursed lips formed a pleasant and easy smile. His eyes became smaller, his skin became perfectly smooth, and his hair became flattened and pushed directly back, as if it were tucked neatly under a veil. The transformation was somewhat like the action that takes place in Michael Jackson's music video for the song titled "Black or White." He was no longer John. I knew that I was looking at Mary. I was looking at our Blessed Mother.

I was mesmerized. She is beautiful. Not like our stereotype of beauty in modern America. She was simply beautiful. Her small eyes were reminiscent of a woman's eyes with no makeup or eye shadow; but the skin and area around Her eyes were perfect, devoid of the marks and shadows most women seek to cover with the very makeup that makes their eyes look bigger and sometimes brighter. I kept looking at Her smile. It was pleasant; Her lips were together, so I could not see Her teeth. Her mouth was small, and Her smile was so slight that it caused no creases in Her cheeks, yet I knew from Her smile that She loves me very much. I don't know how long She was present with me, but for some time, I forgot that Her presence was in the same place that John used to stand. I could feel that I was smiling back at Her. I was calm and happy and so very satisfied to be in Her presence. I did not want that moment to end.

Mary continued to gently sway left to right and back again, just like John was doing. I cannot tell you what She was wearing or even if Her body was dressed in John's clothes. I was so enamored by Her face that I never stopped looking at it. The room was dimly lit, but as Mary swayed left to right, an intensely white light started to show from behind Her neck. It was almost as if the light was trying to hide behind Mary. When She gently shifted to the right, the light appeared from Her left and then disappeared behind Her. When Mary shifted gently to the left, the light appeared again, this time from Her right, and then disappeared behind Her again. This happened over and over and over again. The light was whiter than the whitest light bulb I have ever seen. It was brighter than the sun. Yet as white and bright and pure as the light was, I was able to look right into it as it appeared from behind Mary's neck, and I did not need to squint, and the light did not hurt my eyes. I was having a great time; it was euphoric. I did not want it to end. I was not scared; I was not wondering at all what was happening or why this was happening. I didn't care about any of that. If someone told me that the whole experience lasted thirty seconds or that it lasted thirty minutes, I would believe either. Time seemed not to exist as long as I was in Her presence. It was magical. I never experienced anything like it before, or since. Unless I am blessed to be visited by Mary again, I am quite sure that I will never again experience the simple bliss that I felt while in Her presence—at least not in this lifetime.

As suddenly as the bright light began to appear, it ceased to show itself from behind Mary's neck as She continued to gently sway left to right and back again. Just as in Michael Jackson's video, only in slow motion, Mary's simple beauty turned back into John's familiar face. His eyes were still closed. He was still in prayer. As if he knew that Mary had left my presence, John let go of my hands and took a step away from me. Then John opened his eyes, and my feeling of euphoria slowly faded away. The experience was ended.

There was more to this experience, but that is all I will tell you for now. You will understand the entire experience better once you have gotten to know me and the journey that has been my life. For days and weeks after that experience, I wondered why She chose me to visit. Why then? I had been seeing John for nearly five years. Those thoughts turned into a sense of amazement that I even came to meet John. I thought about John and how he was introduced to me by George. How lucky I was to have met George. How lucky I was that Joe the contractor discouraged us from building a home in Pennsylvania, or I would have never met George. How lucky I was to be alive, and how lucky I was to have met Dr. Mike. There were more "how lucky" thoughts, then I realized that I was not lucky at all. There is no such thing as luck. I had made a series of decisions over the course of my fifty-five years that led me to the very places that would save my life, that would cause me to spend my Wednesday evenings with John. How could I have thought these decisions were all coincidences? I don't know how I could have missed it all those years, but once I pieced these decisions together, they changed my view of how much God actually loves us all. Once I pieced them together, I had new hope and understanding about my future and the paths that I will journey going forward; and once I pieced them together, I knew I needed to write it all down because I knew there must be others who have not figured out that there is no such thing as luck. Good or bad, there is no such thing as luck. There are miracles—miracles that inspire our decisions. That is why I had to write this book.

ACKNOWLEDGMENTS

I wrote this book because after a deeply spiritual and personal encounter with our Blessed Mother, I came to realize that my life is a story that needed to be told. More precisely, the story of six particular decisions that I made and the life path that those decisions created needed to be shared. My life path is a story of the ordinary and the extraordinary, a story of free will and of choices. It is a story of divine guidance. It is a story about the triumph of hope over despair. It is a story of lessons to be learned not just for me, but for you as well, because it is a story about God's love, not just for me, but for us all. My story would not be, but for the love and support of so many special people in my life.

I would like to thank my devoted wife, April, and my wonderful daughters, Christina and Madeline. Most of us hope and expect that our families will return the love and devotion that we share with them. When you are severely ill and unable to contribute to your family as they are accustomed and the love and support they give to you is at that time multiplied one-thousand-fold, it is then that you come to realize what love really is. I have experienced that love, and I am eternally grateful.

My life would not be what it is—it would not be at all—without my mom and dad. Through their love, support, devoted parenting, and their family businesses, they taught me nearly every lesson I needed to succeed in my life and in my career. They taught me that when you fall and hurt your knee, you rub dirt on it, and you move on. I am blessed that when I became ill, my mom was still here with us. At the age of eighty-two, she still had the ability and fortitude to remind me how to rub dirt on it and move on. Thanks, Mom, for still being there when I needed your strength.

I have never written much of anything in my entire life. As you can imagine, my first draft of this book was pretty rough. My brother Domenick contributed hours of time reading and reviewing and helping me to make the stories in this book interesting for you to read without distorting the integrity of their content or messages. For his contribution to this project, I am extremely grateful.

I am truly blessed to have met John Carroll. I know him as a friend, but through the hundreds of hours he has counseled me, he has become my teacher and my healer. He has taught me how to be a more loving husband and a more patient father. He has taught me tolerance and acceptance. He has taught me how my mind can heal my body. He is responsible for the most spiritual and personal encounter I have ever experienced. Thanks, John, for being my friend.

I owe a deep debt of gratitude to Northwell Health and to the executives, doctors, nurses, and administrators who are responsible for the innovation and the caring that happens every day at this incredible institution. I especially thank the surgeons and caregivers that cared for me after my diagnosis and continue to care for me today. Stewardship over such a large and complex organization is an awesome responsibility. Northwell Health is the place where I have advanced my career, it is the place where I have made so many friends, and it is the place that saved my life.

Above all, I thank God. He is the source of all good and our strength to fight all evil. He gave us all the awesome gift of free will and has inspired me to make decisions throughout my life that prepared me for my most difficult moments, days, weeks, and months. I have seen His love and benefited with bounty from His compassion. Because of His inspirations, I have chosen hope over despair; and because of Him, I was compelled to write this book so that others faced with that very same choice can know that hope is the answer.

MIRACLES

This book is not for everyone. In fact, it might not be for you.

It is a book about multiple miracles, all of which happened to me. Now, I am not a student of theology or scripture, nor am I an expert in miracles or divine intervention. It is certainly not my intention to use a term reserved for some of the most extraordinary phenomena experienced by humanity—that have been confirmed by the highest leaders in organized religions—and use that term improperly. So to be clear, let me first explain what I mean when I use the word miracle. As you will see, for purposes of this book, my use of the term is somewhat narrower than you might find if you looked up its definition.

I was raised a Roman Catholic, and I greatly love and respect my religion and my beliefs. One of those beliefs is that each and every one of us was created with a free will, and so whenever we come to a decision we need to make, we are free to choose. Big decisions and small ones, the ones we make dozens, if not hundreds, of times per day, and those we think of as life decisions that require thoughtful consideration and maybe even some analysis. When I use the term miracle, I am referring to certain times in my life when I was faced with a decision. Since I had free will, I could have made a decision in that moment that might have had negative or even detrimental impact on my life. How would I know? Even when they seem small, none of us can understand all the direct and indirect impacts of the decisions we make. I have concluded that in those moments, God intervened, manipulating the timing of events, the circumstances surrounding my decision, or other factors that influenced the decision I actually made. God influenced me to make the "right" decision without ever compromising my free will. The "right" decision? That decision which would prepare me for challenges that I would encounter later in my life—challenges for which such preparation proved fundamental to my ability to endure. That is, as I use the term throughout this book, a miracle. I have experienced multiple miracles that have unquestionably shaped who I am, and even the fact that I am still alive. I want to share these miracles, so you can possibly come to understand how God is using miracles to help you through your own life.

There are several things that I have learned and come to believe about life. I have come to think of them as basic truths. You should understand these basic truths before we begin. Consider the following:

1. *There is a God.* I do not strive to prove that to anyone, but I have come to be utterly and unchangeably convinced that this is a fact. You don't need to believe what I believe in order to find value in the pages of this book. You don't even need to want to be convinced. But you do need to understand that this is fundamental to what I describe to you in these pages. If you do not believe, prepare to be challenged.

2. *God intervenes.* He routinely performs miracles for us. I am not necessarily talking about the unexplainable healing of the sick or bringing people back from the dead. While I do believe that these extraordinary things happen, the vast majority of us will live our entire lives without witnessing any such phenomena. What I am talking about are the miracles that have influenced my decisions and prepared me for significant challenges that were ahead—challenges I never could have imagined at the time I made the deci-

sions. I refer to these events as *miracle-inspired decisions*. These have happened to me, and I think if you consider the events I share with you in these pages, you will find that they have happened to you as well.

3. *Our life follows a path that is blazed by a series of miracle-inspired decisions.* As I have already stated, we make dozens, if not hundreds, of decisions every day. Sometimes we consider those decisions to be significant enough to be life decisions. Often, we reserve for that category such decisions as career choices, selection of our life partner, or the purchase of our home. In fact, we don't know which decisions are the big ones. We may make a quick decision on what appears to be a relatively unimportant matter, only to find many years later that the decision we made was far more meaningful than we ever dreamed possible. I am sure every one of us have considered ourselves "lucky" for a decision we made at some point in our past.

I do not believe in luck. In actuality, I have found that my life has been shaped by a series of decisions that seemed relatively simple at the time; each of those decisions were in and of themselves relatively inconsequential. However, by their nature as a decision that needed to be made, they were a figurative fork in the road where I needed to select a path. God inspired that selection through a miracle. The path I selected led me to another fork in the road that only existed on that path, and with the help from another miracle, I selected another path that brought me to yet another fork in the road, which required another decision that led to yet another path. It is the linkage of these decisions, each influenced by a miracle, that has created my life path. That life path was inspired by God to prepare me for the most challenging times that were to come in my life. In the pages of this book, I have explained the miracles that I have been able to identify in my life and also explained to the best of my ability how the decisions that have been influenced by those miracles are inextricably linked together, creating my life path. I believe you are journeying on your own miracle-inspired life path.

4. *It takes patience to understand miracles and life paths.* In the chapters that follow, I will share six distinct miracles in my life. In order to understand the significance of each and their linkage, I will need to provide you some background on my childhood, my high school and college life, and the events around each miracle-inspired decision. Each of the decisions I describe will seem relatively insignificant on its own. In order for you to understand their collective significance, you will need to be patient and wait until you have learned about most, if not all, of the six miracles I describe. You may find my details to be tedious at times. I assure you that I am providing only what you need to know in order to appreciate the miracle, the miracle-inspired decision, and the linkage. Even after you have understood mine, I think it will be equally challenging for you to chart the life path that God's miracles have created for you.

5. *There is nothing more powerful in life than trust in God and hope for the future.* This is possibly the most important message you can take from the pages that follow. Once I was able to comprehend how God works through miracle-inspired decisions and realized that these miracles are not simply single events but have been linked together to create my life path, I came to understand that I am never alone. God is always there guiding me. I found a new trust in God, a genuine belief that while He might allow me to falter if I so choose, He will always inspire me to choose what is best. That trust has created within me a new hope for my future—a hope that assures me that only good will come my way. Sure, there will be difficult times that I will desire to avoid, but I am utterly confident that even in those times, my miracle-inspired decisions will carry me through to better times. I will share more about trust and hope toward the end of these pages, including how my trust in God and hope for the future has, seemingly ironically,

prepared me for my own death. I believe that your reading of my story will ignite that same trust and hope within you.

I wish now to return to the first sentences of this chapter: *This book is not for everyone. In fact, it might not be for you.* If you believe in God and miracles and are interested in exploring how His profound works may have influenced your life and how they could influence your life in the future, you will likely enjoy reading these chapters and could find comfort and motivation from what I have experienced and learned. If you are not sure if you believe that there is a God—even if you know that you do not—but are open to hearing the experiences of someone who is convinced that we are not walking through this life alone, I believe that your investment of time in the pages that follow will cause you to think and wonder and reflect on the portion of your life that you have lived and the possibilities for the remainder of your life to come. If you have made up your mind that there is no God or that the God that does exist has no intention of guiding you through life's difficult times and life-altering decisions, there is a reasonable chance that you will find my explanation of the miracles that have affected my life to be a boring accounting of a very average life. I still encourage you to give a chapter or two a read. You never know.

One more point before I begin my story. You do not know me yet, but I have already made some aggressive statements about my life. I have told you that I have written this book because I have been influenced by miracles that have *"unquestionably shaped who I am and the fact that I am still alive."* I have also told you that my decisions have created a life path, and *"that life path was inspired by God to prepare me for the most challenging times that were to come in my life."* While you will learn much about who I am and what these statements mean in the pages of this book, some background is warranted before we go any further.

As I write these words, it is spring of 2018. I am fifty-five years old. I am a cancer patient. Note that I have not described myself as a cancer survivor but as a cancer patient. My doctors have assured me that I will be on medications for the rest of my life to keep my condition under control. I have plans to prove them wrong. In July of 2012, very nearly six years ago, I was diagnosed with stage four of a relatively rare cancer. It had metastasized to my lungs and later, to my brain. I underwent an extremely complex surgery less than a week after my diagnosis as I was given three months to live if my surgery was not immediate. I spent twelve days in the hospital, nearly five months recovering at home, and a full year slowly regaining my strength and stamina. Dr. Mike, my surgeon, was confident that I would survive the surgery but made it clear that there was a possibility that I could expire during the procedure. Even with a wildly successful surgery, my life expectancy would be approximately three years. The majority of people with my condition passed away sooner; a minority lived longer.

In a few short months, I will be six years out of surgery. By all accounts, I am doing extremely well. I feel strong and healthy, and the progression of my condition is under control. Any metastases, even the originally diagnosed condition, have come with limited to no symptoms. By all accounts I live a very normal and I would even describe it as a charmed life. I have learned to overcome the challenge of receiving and coping with a life-threatening diagnosis. Blessed with a strong, loving, and supportive family whom you will meet later and a tremendous network of friends, I have moved past the emotional and psychological impact of staring my own mortality in the eyes at the age of forty-nine. The progression of my condition—or lack thereof—is difficult to predict, but I am confident that I have plenty of life ahead of me, a portion of which I have devoted to supporting other cancer patients as they receive and learn to cope with their own potentially life-threatening diagnoses and related treatment decisions.

As a result of one of my miracle-inspired decisions, I have a new perspective on life, a richer and more fulfilling relationship with my wife, April, and my daughters, Christina and Madeline. In so many ways, because of what I have learned and how I have allowed these learnings to affect my approach to life, these past nearly six years have been some of the most joyful, fulfilling, and complete years of my life. Were my life to end tomorrow, I can honestly say that I have lived a wonderful life, and the last six years of it have been the most fulfilling. All because of six miracle-inspired decisions.

Now, read my story. Learn why I am convinced that I am not alone and how I gained new trust and hope for the future; perhaps you will see God's inspirations in your own life.

CHAPTER

2

THE FIRM

T he first miracle-inspired decision I can remember occurred when I was twenty-one. I don't know if one ever happened before that—one might have. But as I have thought about where I am in my life, where my paths have taken me, and track those paths backward, they seem to begin with a decision that I made when I was twenty-one. Before you can appreciate the significance of that decision, or for that matter, the significance of any of the miracle-inspired decisions I will explain, you need to understand a bit about who I am. You need to understand a bit about my family, how I was raised, what motivated me, and what I thought I wanted out of life. So we will begin at the beginning.

I was born in Brooklyn, New York, in 1962 of strong Italian descent. Three of my four grandparents were born in Italy. All four of them had their roots in Naples. Both of my parents' families were passionate and successful entrepreneurs. Mom's family was in the lumber business during a time when Brooklyn and virtually all of the boroughs of New York City were literally under construction, with field after open field being converted to neatly designed square city blocks lined with new homes. They found success for decades, supplying lumber and building materials to a growing city.

Dad's family was in the food business. My grandfather imported Italian provisions and delivered them across the borough. Later, he and his seven sons—he and my grandmother also had six daughters—converted their small warehouse up the block from the family home into a supermarket: Danza Supermarket. It was full service: dry and canned goods, fresh produce, frozen food, deli, and butcher. A progressive approach to food sales in the early 1900s. As the family grew, so did the business. At its peak, the family owned five supermarkets, as well as several other successful businesses. It was in the supermarkets that I learned so much about life, people, and business, and so it is in those supermarkets that we will spend some time together.

We were an extraordinarily traditional Italian family. My father and his brothers—I will refer to them as the seven sons—and their six sisters were extremely close. As they grew up and got married, they all settled into homes within a few miles of each other, partly because so many of them needed to be close to the businesses but also because everyone wanted to be a short drive from the hub, the home of my grandparents. Whenever we visited that home, we were sure to find others from the family also there. It is where I came to know my uncles and aunts and my cousins. Before I was a teenager, I had more than sixty cousins. My dad always told me that I didn't need friends. "Friends come and go, but your cousins will be your cousins forever." He was right. Of course, I have found some wonderful friends over the years, but those cousins that I came to know and trust from the earliest age I can remember are my friends for life.

We were devout Catholics. We went to Catholic grade schools, which were part of the Catholic churches that my uncles and aunts supported during their construction and renovations. We were taught by nuns and priests who were often guests at our Sunday dinner tables. My grandparents, all of my thirteen aunts and uncles, and many of their spouses spoke Italian. Amazingly, none of them had Italian accents, and while you could hear it spoken in every one of their households, it was never taught to me or any of my cousins. That's because my grandparents were also proud to be Americans. They took a very different approach to immigration than seems so prevalent today. They felt privileged to be accepted into America, and raising their children and grandchildren in the mainstream American culture seemed to be the best way to assure our integration and success. With very little education, even they seemed to be able to shed their Italian accents for the more contemporary "Brooklynese." Still, they carried forward many of their Italian customs.

Every Christmas was celebrated at the hub. It was an all-day affair. We were all there, and as the cousins started to get married their spouses and children were always welcome. There was more than one Christmas where my grandparents probably hosted close to one hundred people for ante pasto, sit down dinner, dessert, presents—each of the dozens of grandchildren got one gift—and the recitation of the rosary. The family functioned around the hub, and the hub thrived because of the business.

The seven sons were the most astute businesspeople I have ever met. I have often said that my college education was just a formality because I learned everything I needed to succeed in the business world from the time I spent in those supermarkets. I never truly understood how they became such amazing businessmen. Most of them never finished high school, and none of them graduated college; but they were quite impressive, each and every one of them. By the time I was ten, I was spending time in the supermarkets; we called them the stores. I don't know what it is like to take a snow day off from school because Dad always took me to the store. I spent many of my summer weekdays there as well. He always told me that he needed me to work, and it wasn't until years later that I realized he was just looking to keep me off the streets and out of trouble. I didn't mind. I liked watching my father run the store. He seemed to enjoy the customers, the workers, the energy that permeated the ten thousand square foot structure when it got busy with shoppers. In those early years, for my pay, I was able to walk around the store and pick a favorite food to take home. I usually picked the chocolate pop tarts.

By the time I was fourteen, I was ready to graduate from pop tarts to a paying job in one of the stores, but it was not to be the one that my father managed. You see, when a niece or nephew was old enough to begin to work, they spend their apprentice years working for someone other than their father. It was almost the right of passage. I went across town to work for Uncle Eddie for the next two summers. I enjoyed my time with Uncle Eddie. He was younger than my dad, about twenty years older than me. He was a tough boss; I think that was part of the apprenticeship. I learned the fundamentals of the business. I worked a lot in the fresh produce department, learning how to identify the most tasty and sweet fruits and vegetables. I unloaded trucks, and I packed the shelves. Importantly, I learned what it meant to work an intense ten-hour day. Even more important than that, I learned how to treat and respect the customer. You see, Uncle Eddie might have been a tough boss, but he could tolerate honest mistakes. He didn't get mad when I dropped a case of soda that broke all over the floor or when I forgot to put the extra milk in the dairy refrigerator. However, he would not tolerate my walking past a customer who was looking for something without asking if I could help or not saying hello to a regular customer who he introduced to me the week before. To this day, I believe that respectful service to the customer is the most important business lesson I have ever learned.

I was sixteen and finishing up my sophomore year of high school. I made the bold move of asking my dad if I could work that upcoming summer in his store. He didn't answer right away; I think he needed to talk to his brothers. In short order, I was spending that next summer—and after school and every other subsequent summer until I was a junior in college—driving with my dad to Canarsie, Brooklyn, to work with him in his store. It was during these four years that I came to learn how the business actually worked. The Canarsie store was run by my dad and Uncle Vinnie. Uncle Vinnie was the youngest of the seven sons and had a very different management style from my dad. I learned from both of them, and I came to respect different management styles and to realize that each could effectively achieve the business goals. During my years in Canarsie, I worked in virtually every department in the store. In addition to the departments I learned from Uncle Eddie, I worked in the deli, ran the cash registers, and drove the van, delivering groceries to customers' homes. On a busy Saturday, we would get at least 150 deliveries.

I never worked so hard in my life, and I don't think I ever worked that physically hard ever again. I also learned the dynamics of the business, how the business made money. It was eloquently simple to understand but incredibly complex to master. As I had learned from Uncle Eddie, it was all about the customer. My dad taught me to treat them like queens; in the late '70s and early '80s, 90 percent of supermarket customers were women. Make them feel important, and they come back. Make them feel like they are nobody, and they go to Waldbaum's, our biggest competitor. Stock items they ask for and run specials for their holidays, and they buy more. Understand who they are and who their kids are and where they work and why they are happy or unhappy today, and they will become loyal customers for life. And that is what this family business did: we created loyal customers for life. Why? Because it was right to treat people well. Why else? Because customers gave you the money, and the money was the revenue. When you collect more revenue, you grow. When you hire the right employees and you manage your vendors and your inventory and your pricing and you know how to manage your utility and occupancy costs, you make profit. Eloquently simple to understand. Incredibly complex to master, and it all starts with the customer. These were lessons I would take with me throughout my business career—lessons that could be applied to every business, whether you sold products or provided services. I absolutely loved it. I decided by my junior year of college that I would somehow run a business. It was my passion, and the ability to manage the factors— from customers to costs—was an exhilarating art, especially when there were profits left over at the end. Yes, it was rewarding to create loyal customer, and it was noble to reward competent employees, but it was exhilarating to earn profits. And for-profit, entrepreneurism was my career aspiration.

I was an accounting major at New York University, and by my junior year of college I had earned an internship at a medium-sized public accounting firm. So my career in the supermarkets was ending. The lessons would live on forever. By the winter of 1984, I was twenty-one, and I would be graduating from NYU in a few months. It was interview season, and my career objective was set: get an interview at as many of the "Big 8" public accounting firms as I could; land a job at one of these prestigious firms; make partner; sell and deliver quality services; create loyal clients; get rich; retire early. Eloquently simple to understand. Incredibly complex to master, but I was sure that I could convert what my dad and my uncles taught me into a successful career in public accounting.

In 1984, the Big 8 were the eight largest and most prestigious global accounting firms in the world. They were, in alphabetical order: Arthur Andersen, Coopers and Lybrand, Deloitte Haskins and Sells, Ernst and Whinney, Peat Marwick Mitchell, Price Waterhouse, Touch Ross, and Arthur Young. Landing a job with any one of them was key to getting my career started on the right foot. I was off to a great start. By early spring, I had secured interviews with all of the firms. By the time I had interviewed with seven of the eight, I had received offers from six of the seven to become a new staff accountant. Exciting. All the starting salaries were close—either $19,000 or $19,500. I very much liked Price Waterhouse. They had a high-end feel. Their offices felt like expensive law offices with lots of polished wood and shiny clean tiled floors. There was an air about them that was proud, confident. It was almost arrogant. I could sell business and make money there. I also liked Arthur Young. Their culture was far more laid-back. While their offices were most certainly professional, they were casual compared to those of Price Waterhouse. I liked these people. I could sell and make money here too. One more interview and then my decision. Yes, the first decision I can remember that would be miracle inspired.

My interview with Arthur Andersen was scheduled for March 15. The interview process had been long and tiring, and I wasn't really looking forward to this last interview. I had gotten offers from six of the Big 8. I found two firms that I liked and that liked me. I could be successful at either of these firms. Did I really need to do this anymore? I was prepared to cancel my interview with Arthur Andersen and accept the offer from one of the other two firms. My only hesitation was whether it was a wise career move to tell one of the Big 8 firms that I was not interested in meeting them. Would I ever cross their path again in the future? Would they remember me? I thought that would be the issue of the week.

Then we got the news; it moved swiftly through the family. He had been sick, so we should not have been surprised. It would just have been a matter of time. The time was now. Still, we were all stunned; and since nothing like this had ever happened this close in the family, at least in my lifetime, many of us were not sure what to do or how to react. My grandfather had passed away. The man who fathered this large, close-knit clan, the man who started the family business out of the back of a delivery truck, the man who was the king of the hub was gone. He was really gone. Naturally, the seven sons and their six sisters had many details to tend to. Making sure my grandmother was comforted was job one. It was only a day or so later that many of the plans were in place. The wake would start in another two days and last for three more long and difficult ones. The funeral and burial would be the following day—on March 15. That's right. March 15. That was the same day as my interview. There was another very big decision that had also been made. The stores would remain open on the day of the funeral. After careful consideration, the seven sons concluded that their father would have wanted it that way. After all, the family thrived because of the business. There was only one problem: Who would tend to the stores that day? Of course, the seven sons would attend the funeral mass and the burial, but there was one business rule that was very rarely, if ever, broken. At least one of the seven sons was always present in each of the stores whenever they were open. Period. For this extraordinary occasion, the seven sons decided that they would rely on a handful of the nephews to manage the stores in their absence. Uncle Eddie was the brother that called me to let me know they had decided that I would manage his store that day. This was not a request or a suggestion. It was a decision they had made that was my obligation to fulfill. I agreed. Not only was it an obligation, but it was an honor. To be trusted to be "in charge" of one of the stores from opening to its closing was a rare and awesome responsibility that was not to be taken lightly. It expressed a level of trust and confidence that, until that moment, I had no way of knowing that any of the seven sons, even my dad, had for me.

So it was done. I would miss the funeral and work in the store that day. Oh, and I also had the perfect excuse to cancel my interview at Arthur Andersen. And so I did. It worked out just fine. How could it not? When I contacted the recruiter at Arthur Andersen and explained my situation, she was most understanding. "Don't worry about the interview. I hope everything goes as well as it can."

The three days of the wake were long and tiring. I had classes in the morning then afternoon and evening wake hours that ended at 10:00 p.m. Each day and evening, the funeral home overflowed with literally hundreds of members of the extended family, neighbors, friends, and of course, loyal customers who came to pay their respects. Each night after the wake, the entire family—dozens and dozens of us—went back to the hub. Until midnight or so, each of those nights, we comforted each other, came to grips with what was happening, and found a way to laugh a little together. Then came the day of the funeral.

I showed up about fifteen minutes early for the 8:00 a.m. opening of the store. I pulled up the gates, turned on the lights, completed the customary walk through of the store that happened every morning before any customers came in, and let the process begin. Employees filed in on time. The lights in the deli case were turned on, and in a few short minutes it was filled with potato salad, coleslaw, and other fresh favorites and was ready for business. Cashiers were at their registers. The butcher department lights were lit, and the butcher was filling its refrigerated case with freshly cut steaks, chicken, and sausage. The stock boys filed in and began to place the morning's milk delivery into the dairy case. Finally, the customers started to arrive. Everyone in the store understood the significance of this day, and each and every one of them wanted to be a part of a successful day—for Uncle Eddie. It was an uneventful and successful day at the store; I was very thankful.

The funeral mass was to start at 10:00 a.m. In keeping with the traditions of the day, after the mass, the hearse and the entire funeral procession would drive past the locations that were most important in the life of the deceased. That meant a drive past the hub and then past each of the five stores. Every employee in the store was keeping one eye out the window starting around 11:00 a.m. Nobody wanted to miss this. At around 11:30 a.m., one of the cashiers yelled across the store, "They're here!" They locked the cash registers, and every employee was out on the sidewalk just as the hearse paused in front of the store. The customers didn't mind. In fact, most of them left their grocery carts in place and joined us on the now crowded sidewalk. I looked up and realized that it was not only the store that had emptied. The storefronts on either side of the store and across the avenue had also emptied, employees and customers filling the sidewalks. It more resembled a parade than a funeral procession, except the avenue was completely silent. With a tear in my eye, I said a prayer and then made the sign of the cross. The funeral procession quietly started up again, and as it disappeared down the avenue, everyone returned to wherever it was that they were just a few minutes earlier. Everything was back to normal. It was one of the most memorable couple of minutes I have ever experienced. I remember it as if it had happened ten minutes ago. That was nearly thirty-five years ago.

Things would never be the same again after that day, but slowly the family returned to normal, albeit a new normal. I began to look forward to graduation. I would accept one of those offers, get finals behind me, and enjoy one more summer before I started my new career in public accounting. This summer would not include working in the stores. That was a little bittersweet.

A couple of nights after the funeral, the phone rang. There was no caller ID in 1984, or I may not have ever even picked up the phone. I said hello, and it was the partner in charge of recruitment at Arthur Andersen: the partner, Allen. Allen introduced himself, conveyed his condolences, and asked me how I was doing. I was absolutely floored. After a brief and friendly discussion, Allen invited me in for the interview that I had to cancel just a few days earlier. I explained to him that I had made my mind up to accept an offer at one of the competing firms. I almost remember his response verbatim: "Frank, we still have a few starting positions open for this season. I have personally reviewed your file, and I think that you have what it takes to succeed here. I also think you would be a terrific fit. Why not come in and meet some members of our team and see for yourself." What was I supposed to say? No? To the partner? So as professionally as I knew how, I agreed to come for the interview but assured him that my mind was made up.

The interview was just a few days later. I got up and dressed in my interview suit, but my heart was not in it. I really did not want to go. A short subway ride later, I was in midtown Manhattan and checking in for my interview. The offices were nice. The traditional wooden Arthur Andersen doors were at every entrance. The space was tastefully done. Not too stuffy, yet not too casual. The people I met were the same: the women in their high-collared suits, the men in their white shirts and red ties—stereotypically Arthur Andersen—but the people were different. A little more like my own perception of myself, or the professional I would like to mature into. Highly professional, but friendly. Extremely confident, but down-to-earth. Book smart, but at the same time, street smart. I must admit that I was impressed, but I was not going to change my mind. I had the traditional schedule of interviews that day. I met a partner, a manager, and a senior accountant then lunch with two staff accountants. One of them was just finishing up his first year, and the other was just finishing up her second. It was a very comfortable lunch. I actually liked these people. So yes, I was starting to think that I could sell work and create loyal clients here too. But I was still not planning to change my mind. After lunch, a final interview with human resources. That is when I met Allen. He was a little older than I was picturing, donned a white shirt and red tie, and was also very friendly. It was the end of the interview season, so Allen got right to business. He explained that all of the folks I met thought the discussions had gone well and that they were prepared to make me an offer. Drum roll please: $19,500. Did these firms have each other on speed dial? I thanked him and, as was customary, told him I needed to think about it. Then I shook his hand and headed home.

If it was not that night, it was the very next night when the phone rang again. It was Allen. I started to say, "Hi Allen, I am glad you called, I was..." I wanted to tell him that I was going to call him the next day to let him know that I would be sticking to my original decision and would not be accepting his offer. He must have sensed it because he professionally interjected before I could go any further. He explained that they had reviewed the starting salaries for the new class of staff accountants and decided that they had misread the market. As a result, he was prepared to increase my offer from $19,500 to $20,500; $20,500—they pierced the $20,000 price point. Impressive.

To this day I can't tell you why, but it was as if he had just tripled the offer. It was as if he was calling to tell me I had won the lottery. Come on, it was one thousand dollars! Regardless, it worked. It all worked. The call from a partner, the lunch with the two staff people, the modest salary increase that seemed so large because the new number started with a two, it all worked. With hardly a pause I said, "Allen, your offer is very generous. I accept your offer, and I am excited to get started."

Accept his offer? What had I just done? There was no way that I could be excited to get started; I wasn't even planning to start at his firm! I was not the kind of person that changed his mind. In fact, to this day, I am a little on the hardheaded side. The words came out, and I could not get them back. Funny thing is that after I hung up the phone, I had no buyer's remorse. I didn't have it the next day either or the next week or the next month. I had no buyer's remorse when I got on the plane to head to Illinois for new staff training. The moment I hung up the phone, I knew it was the right decision. I didn't know why; I just knew. My interview process was complete. I would start at Arthur Andersen on August 1. I had made one of the biggest decisions of my relatively young life. I didn't know it at the time, but it was also the first miracle-inspired decision that I would remember in my later years. As you will see in future chapters, I had selected the only firm that would force me to abandon my plan and get onto a path that would eventually save my life.

CHAPTER

3

HEALTHCARE

$\mathbf{A}$ decade went by before the next miracle-inspired decision—at least the next one that I can remember. In the meantime, I had a career to build, loyal clients to create, and an early retirement for which to save.

My career at Arthur Andersen started on August 1, 1984. It began with a week of orientation in the local Manhattan office then off to the firm's training center in St. Charles, Illinois. The training center was in the middle of nowhere, an hour-plus drive from Chicago and about the same distance from O'Hare International Airport. The facility, in the middle of corn fields and open space, still looked and functioned like the small college campus that it once was. I slept in a tiny dorm room complete with a roommate from South America. We could barely communicate but somehow managed to share our cramped quarters for the subsequent two weeks. We ate our meals in what amounted to a college cafeteria and then, like a line of ants, walked across the small grassy campus to spend the next twelve straight days performing a simulated audit in outdated college classrooms. The training was intense and effective. The facility would receive a complete makeover in the years to come, but what foresight the leaders of this firm had to commit time and significant financial resources to a facility dedicated to such comprehensive training. No other firm had anything like it. I started to think that my last-minute decision to join Arthur Andersen was a good one.

Before I left the training center to head home, I received a call from the staffing department back in Manhattan and learned that I had been assigned to my first client. I would report to the client site on the Monday morning right after my return from St. Charles—no need to even stop off in the Manhattan office. This was great. When you are a brand-new employee in an incredibly competitive environment, you look for any indication that you are doing as well or better than your peers. I was one of the first staff members from my starting class to get assigned. Good sign. Well, not really, but I genuinely thought so at the time. I was pleased nonetheless to know that I would begin serving my first client immediately upon my return to New York.

Monday, August 20. I had set my alarm clock for 6:00 a.m. but was awake over an hour before it rang. I tossed around a short while until it was clear that my sleep was ended. Never my best in the morning, I was not surprised at all that I was even less capable when fumbling around in the predawn darkness. As I showered and completed my morning ritual, I became aware of the butterflies that were beginning to form in my stomach. Just some nervousness, I reassured myself. It will pass. My choice of clothing for the day was easy. My favorite gray pinstriped suit, crisp white shirt, and red tie. Distinctively Arthur Andersen. As I knotted my tie, the butterflies grew into full-blown nausea that would remain with me for the remainder of the morning. This was going to be a long day. It was still rather early when I arrived at the offices of my first client, a very large financial services company located in the financial district, downtown Manhattan. It was a high-profile engagement because it was what was called a "last time through." That meant that the client had told us that this would be the last audit we would be doing for them. It was time for them to select new auditors. Last time through audits are high profile because you know for sure that the next auditors will be looking at your working papers in preparation for their "first time through" the audit. You always want your papers in particularly good shape in such a situation.

The first thing that happened on that first Monday is that I met my first audit senior—my boss, Julie. Julie was tough, no-nonsense, very focused on getting the job done, very focused on making sure the client was satisfied, the audit manager was happy, the timelines were met, and the workpapers were excellent. It was not lost on her that our competitors would be looking at our work in a few short months, and she was not about to become embarrassed by even the smallest detail out of place. Her work ethic was a lot like that of the seven sons. As I came to know and understand Julie and her work ethic, I thought again that my choice to join Arthur Andersen was a good one.

Julie and I have become terrific friends, and nearly thirty-five years later, Julie and her husband, Chris, and me and April are very close. I learned a lot from Julie. I learned how to do the job. I learned about customer service in a professional environment, client service. I learned about working with others in the office setting. Thankfully, I had already learned what it meant to work hard from my days in the stores because this was hard work. We had some tight deadlines, so even as late summer turned into fall—the proverbial slow season in this business—we were working mandatory twelve-hour days. I was also studying for the CPA exam and had classes at Madison Square Garden two nights per week. In order to make those classes and still put in my full work days, I was in by 6:00 a.m., worked until 6:00 p.m., and found my way to the Garden by 7:00 p.m. The prep class ended at 10:00 p.m., and I was home by 11:00 p.m. We also worked some Saturdays and Sundays. It was intense and lasted into January of 1985. My first client engagement was in the books!

As I gained experience and a positive reputation, I was assigned to some of the bigger and more prestigious clients, large publicly-traded companies with complex businesses. They expected excellent service and meticulous attention to detail. They expected us to understand their inventory management practices and identify opportunities to improve their business. I understood from my days in the stores why these things were so important, and I thrived on learning more and more about these businesses and how they worked. The best measure of success is when your client and your partner wanted you back for the following year's audit. I spent multiple years at each of these special clients. I was becoming more confident that my decision to join Arthur Andersen was a good one.

By 1989 I was promoted to manager. Right on schedule. All was good. All was great. Right? Well, almost. Remember my personal goals: "sell and deliver quality service; create loyal clients; get rich; retire early." This work I was doing was a great way to hone my skills and deliver quality service, but I really didn't have the opportunity I was looking for to develop my own business by creating loyal clients. Something was missing. I wanted more.

The 1980s and 1990s were the age of process reengineering. All of the Big 8 firms were establishing consulting practices focused on helping their clients completely change the way they conducted business, including wholesale changes to their organization structures and technologies. Interesting work. A way to build a new business; a chance to create loyal clients. I had an opportunity to get staffed on a project. I liked it. I had the opportunity to transfer into the newly formed Business Consulting Group (we called it BC). I took it. My second miracle-inspired decision? I don't think so. This was a logical career move. You will see how a decision I made later in this chapter was much more counterintuitive—that one required some inspiration.

Transferring into BC satisfied the last component of my personal plan: create loyal clients. You see, audit was important, but it seemed to me that I was doing the same work for the same clients that had been done by some other auditor the year before, not because the client wanted me to, but because the client was required to have me do it. BC work was very different. These were interesting and creative projects designed to help my client solve a problem. No two problems were the same, and so every project was a unique challenge. Clients viewed their consultants differently than they did their auditors. They chose to hire their consultants; nobody required them to do it. So the dynamic was different. They were paying for our insights and ideas and recommendations. Our work was actually strategic and important to the business. Fix your client's business problem, and that client became a loyal client. This is what I was looking for. I was quite sure that my decision to join Arthur Andersen was a good one.

BC was where I met Gail. Gail ran BC in the New York office when I joined in 1989; later she would lead the practice globally. I was among the first half dozen or so consultants to join the group in New York. Over the course of the next eleven or so years, the practice grew at a feverish pace, and our number of consultants in the Northeast grew into the hundreds. During that time, Gail was my boss and became a lifelong friend and mentor. There has been no career decision I have made in the past twenty-five-plus years that I did not discuss and receive valuable guidance from Gail.

My time in BC was some of the most rewarding years in my professional career. The 1990s were the years of merger and integration in the health insurance industry. Many of the Blue Cross Blue Shield companies (abbreviated BCBS) across the country were considering mergers; many people do not know that they were all separate insurance companies until the 1990s, most licensed to sell insurance is a single state. Merger work was a perfect next step in the progression of my career; it leveraged my reengineering experience and required additional competencies in organizational design and information technology strategy. I found these areas very interesting and, in some cases, intuitive.

Eric, a senior partner in BC, had some relationships in the health insurance industry, and I was assigned to one of his projects. New Jersey BCBS was considering a merger with New York's Empire BCBS. The merger never happened, but the work we did to support the due diligence performed on behalf of the New Jersey company was fun and interesting. Eric was happy with my work; eventually it was Eric's support, together with Gail's, for my candidacy, that ultimately got me admitted to the partnership. So when these merger opportunities came to our attention, Eric included me on his team. The biggest such assignment was the merger of three BCBS companies—Ohio, Kentucky, and Indiana—to form the company that came to be called Anthem. Anthem has grown since to become one of the largest insurers in the county. Our assignment was to look across the three companies and identify areas for consolidation that would result in cost savings. I worked in the departments that paid claims to hospitals and doctors, enrolled new customers—or members—into Anthem's insurance plans, and received and responded to customer phone calls. Collectively the industry refers to these areas as claims, membership, and service.

Teamed with client personnel, we came up with some creative ideas to integrate the three companies and improve the operations. I became somewhat expert in these specific insurance areas. This was key to my career progression because a year later, when our planning work was complete, Anthem needed to decide how to get these ideas implemented. I was well positioned to sell the "add-on" work, and Eric gave me the latitude to give it my best shot. My first sales opportunity that I ever took the lead on was successful: a multimillion-dollar implementation project. By the time that work was done, I had spent over three years in the Midwest, learned a ton, delivered some high-quality work, and earned a position as partner at Arthur Andersen. I had decided for sure that my decision to join Arthur Andersen was a good one.

Partner. It was 1996, I was thirty-four years old, and I was progressing nicely toward the goals that I had set when I was twenty-one, contemplating which firm I would join. "Sell and deliver quality service...create loyal clients..." I utilized those skills I learned in the Midwest to continue to progress my career. There were other mergers going on in the industry, and if you created a loyal client you could remain at that client for years. This was key because sales and cash collections were the two metrics that every partner needed to deliver in order to be successful. Across the consulting industry, the saying is still used: "you eat what you kill." There was a large merger on the east coast of what was then the two largest behavior health insurance companies in the region. BC was well-known enough in this space that I was invited to the bid. We nailed it. Our credentials could not be matched. "We hired you because you are like the marines. When you bring in BC you get things done. We need to get some things done."

My first years as partner went smoothly, and I was busy selling and delivering quality service and creating loyal clients. It was during that time that I came to know that I was here to stay. I would stay in BC, grow my business, and retire from Arthur Andersen. I used to say that I had checked off the box next to the word "career." Mission accomplished. Decision made. Objective achieved. I was living the dream. Call it what you want. I was around thirty-five, and I had decided what I would do for the rest of my working life.

There is a well-known rule in consulting. Every five years or so, you need to reinvent yourself. CEOs change. Company goals change. Industry trends change. If you stay the same, you get left behind. You get left behind and don't sell any work. Your clients become loyal to someone else. So as the merger mania in the health insurance industry started to cool down, it was time to reinvent myself. Where else, in what other industry were mergers getting hot? I was pretty sure I could convert my skills to another industry. On the other hand, did I want to learn the dynamics of another whole business? Maybe not. Maybe I should figure out the next big thing that health insurance companies were going to buy. I had some planning to do. But my sales were strong, my clients were loyal, and I had some time. I wasn't concerned.

Enter Eric again. He proposed an idea to me that went something like this: "Frank, we are in New York City. There are big hospitals all around us. People come from all over the country, really all over the world to get treated in a New York City hospital. We have no healthcare practice in our region. Since you have some experience in health insurance, I think it makes sense for you to start a healthcare practice. We have big practices in other BC regions, and they have products and services that you can bring here. Think about it. I think you should do it."

Huh. I have health insurance experience. That sounds a lot like healthcare, right? We have people in other regions that have products I can sell. Sounds like a good idea, right? Well, not really. Health insurance sounds like healthcare, but the insurance business is nothing like the hospital business. Not even close. I would need to learn a new business. At the time, there were very few hospitals considering a merger transaction. I did merger and implementation work. I would also need to learn a new service. It made no sense at all for me to try to start a new consulting practice in an industry I did not know with services I had never delivered.

There is more. I didn't like hospitals. They scared me. They smelled like cleaning chemicals and had sick people in them. I had never had an event that required me to be a patient in a hospital, but most of the memories I had of ever being in a hospital was when I needed to visit someone who was sick enough that they were probably not coming home again. The only person I had ever remembered visiting in a hospital that was going to be well enough to come home was when I visited Domenick, my older brother, after he had his appendix removed. I was only a teenager, but when they raised the back of his bed, he winced in pain. My face went pale, and my lips turned white. The nurse had to help me until the room stopped spinning and I was able to stand without leaning on her. I was incredibly embarrassed. I could not wait to get out of there, and I hoped I would never have to go into a hospital again.

As if my fear of hospitals was not enough, doctors also made me nervous. Even the word doctor immediately conjured up thoughts of my childhood trips to our family doctor which were for one of two reasons: because I was sick with an earache or sore throat or fever or because it was time to get a shot. Miserable memories. At the time, I didn't like seeing doctors, being in the same room with them, or talking to them. So I had no good vibes about the healthcare industry.

There is still more. Lou was our office managing partner, Eric's boss. He didn't like hospitals either, for different reasons. The hospitals in our region were either owned by the city or not-for-profit organizations. In Lou's mind, that meant fee discounts and slow payment. He did not support the idea of creating a healthcare practice in his region. To be clear, Lou was a generous man, a big supporter of not-for-profit organizations, just not a fan of building new consulting practices to service them. The firm already had a fairly large practice that serviced not-for-profit companies at fairly steep discounts, mostly in the audit business. There was yet another concern related to building my new business in an industry that was not-for-profit. These hospitals needed to generate enough money to cover their costs, but were they motivated to drive their business to create margin? To create profits—the piece of the business that I found exhilarating? The piece of the business that would cause them to purchase large consulting projects and become loyal clients? Probably not. So after some thought, I decided that this was not a good idea.

I met with Eric on several occasions to discuss his idea and finalize my decision. We talked about the short list of pros and the considerably longer list of cons. Now Eric is soft spoken, not the "hard sell" type. When he sold work to clients, he didn't stand up in front of the room and talk and talk and talk about all the things he knew and how great he and his team was at what they did. He listened. He got the client to talk through their problems. He *facilitated* the client through a discussion that helped them understand how to solve their problem—and how he could help. He was smooth, not slick. But I knew this, and I was not going to get *facilitated* into healthcare. We talked, and I focused on the long list of cons. We talked some more, and I focused some more on the long list of cons. I explained other things I could do, and he focused on the short list of pros. Eric was as much a mentor as he was a boss, so these discussions were not difficult or uncomfortable, but just like I told Allen when he asked me to come for an interview, I was not changing my mind.

It was time to finalize my decision, so Eric came by my office one day and asked me what I had decided. I looked up and paused a minute. I had never considered it before; in the several weeks I had been pondering this decision, I never thought about it quite this way, but in that moment, it dawned on me that Eric was asking me to do this because it was the right thing for BC. "Yes, I will start a healthcare practice."

What? Yes? Why had I said that? Yes was never in any of my rehearsed answers. Just like when I said yes to Allen, I had not planned to say yes. There wasn't even an extra thousand in it for me this time! But this time, I did have some buyer's remorse. For quite some time I wondered if I had made the right decision. I wondered if I should change my mind, but I did not. I didn't know it at the time, but this was my second miracle-inspired decision. I realize you can't see it yet either, but you will shortly.

I spent a fair bit of time with my colleagues in other regions within BC. Eric was right. They had, in fact, developed several services that I could learn and bring back to my clients in the New York area. The product I found most interesting and that I was able to sell most effectively was Revenue Cycle Management. Getting paid for the care you provide in the healthcare industry is complicated. There are literally hundreds of steps required to get paid, and that combination of steps is referred to as the revenue cycle. Revenue Cycle Management was a great product to sell. I helped my clients figure out better ways to perform the hundreds of steps that they needed to complete in order to get paid on each claim, usually for tens or even hundreds of thousands of claims each year. Clients were willing to pay higher fees for revenue cycle projects because there was a clear increase in their cash. They could justify the cost because the projects clearly paid for themselves—and then some. For me, it provided the possibility to sell bigger projects. Even in a small system of three or four hospitals, hundreds of people were required to complete all the work across the revenue cycle. In larger systems, it could involve thousands of employees. My largest client required approximately three thousand employees to perform the revenue cycle for its hospitals and doctors. The revenue cycle was big operations, and big operations call for big consulting projects. So Revenue Cycle Management was one of my favorite products.

Over the course of the first couple of years, I learned to sell and deliver Revenue Cycle Management and other healthcare products, built a small group of consultants capable of delivering these services, and started to build a small group of loyal clients. They were mostly individual hospitals or small systems comprised of a handful of hospitals. They were all not-for-profit or government organizations. As I anticipated, the world of not-for-profit was very different than the for-profit clients I was used to. Even when I was selling Revenue Cycle Management, these clients were a little more cautious, not so quick to spend on a larger consulting engagement even when the return on investment was clear. Many people I met in healthcare didn't even understand the concept and fundamentals of a return on investment. This was the '90s. A lot has changed since then. So I would describe my early years consulting in the healthcare industry as just reasonably successful. Lou was right. Most of the projects were small, and most of the payments were slow.

In 1998, I met Bob, the Chief Financial Officer (CFO) of the North Shore-Long Island Jewish Health System (NSLIJ). NSLIJ was a large not-for-profit health system headquartered on Long Island in New York. They employed hundreds of doctors and owned sixteen hospitals. They were big. And so was their revenue cycle. Bob heard from his peers in the industry that BC could help him improve his revenue cycle, and Bob hired me to get it done. At that point, it was the largest revenue cycle project we had ever delivered, and we exceeded Bob's expectations. Over the course of the next couple of years, we did a variety of projects for Bob. NSLIJ became an important client to me, and I always considered it to be a unique and special place. Bob became a loyal client. To this day, I have maintained a strong relationship with Bob.

NSLIJ eventually changed its name to Northwell Health, and from now on, I will refer to that health system as Northwell.

With Northwell as one of my best clients and Revenue Cycle Management my best service, the healthcare practice I had started continued to grow at a slow but steady pace. I still questioned how I had ended up in this somewhat odd industry. I still wondered if I had made the right decision. Then one day in 2001, the unthinkable happened. Arthur Andersen was in trouble. It was being reported in every media outlet, on every television channel. A client I had never heard of, called Enron, had collapsed, and Arthur Andersen was the auditor. Billions of dollars of value had been lost from shareholder investment accounts and employee retirement accounts. There were accusations and indictments. Eventually there would be depositions, trials, and suicides. Arthur Andersen had completed its audit just months earlier and took much of the blame. This book is not about who was right or who was wrong. I don't even know enough of the details to form an intelligent opinion. What I do know is that in a matter of months, Arthur Andersen was gone. The loyal clients, the eighty thousand employees worldwide—gone.

Let's pause because a lot has happened so far. At twenty-one, I made a miracle-inspired decision to join Arthur Andersen. As the years passed, I became confident that I had made a sound decision. I had found the place where I planned to work for the rest of my career. I genuinely believe I would have been successful at any of the Big 8 I might have joined. They all had great audit clients. They all rewarded entrepreneurs who were able to create loyal clients, and very importantly, they all moved into the consulting business at the same time. I could have had a similar career at any of the firms. What was different about Arthur Andersen? It was the only one of the Big 8—the only one of the seven firms that made me an offer—that met its demise during my career. It was the only one of the firms I had to choose from that literally forced me to leave, forced me to exit my comfort zone and find another career. The only firm that forced me to find another career after I had "checked the box" near the very word career and decided I was staying in BC.

But where would I go? Where would the next step in my career take me? Well, that is the topic of another chapter: the result of another miracle-inspired decision. For now, let's remember that as a result of the second miracle-inspired decision that I can remember, I had developed this skill set in Revenue Cycle Management, in—of all industries—not-for-profit health care.

CHAPTER 4

NORTHWELL

I am a decisive person. I think through my decisions fairly thoroughly, at least the ones that I consider to be important. I don't typically overanalyze things; I don't like to take weeks—certainly not months—to make even the biggest of decisions.

Arguably, one of the biggest decisions any of us ever makes is the selection of our life partner. I met April in July of 1986. We were engaged by July of 1987. Once I began to believe that April was "the one," I thought about it seriously for a month, possibly a little longer, and then I "popped the question." That is how I generally make decisions. Over the course of my career, I have been responsible for making decisions that involve large investments in technology and operating expenses with the potential for fairly large returns on those investments. I have proposed that we make investments of tens of millions of dollars with expected returns on those investments in very short time frames, in many cases a year or less. I study these investment opportunities thoroughly. But I study them for weeks, not for months. Once I have made the decision, I speak with conviction about the benefits, present fair disclosure about the risks, and position a strong and convincing argument to move forward. I can say that throughout my career, I have made dozens of such proposals, the majority of which have been funded/approved, the vast majority of which have met or exceeded their objectives. My point? Within my life and scope of responsibilities, I generally study my alternatives thoroughly but relatively quickly. I guess I get bored easily. Once I have made a decision, I stick by it. I relentlessly make the decision work. April and I have been happily married for nearly thirty years; admittedly, she deserves more credit than I do, but the fact still remains. My business proposals generally achieve or exceed their stated objectives and returns.

I have been told that I am hardheaded, stubborn, and controlling. I suppose that I am. That is what makes the miracle-inspired decisions that I can remember happening throughout my life so profound. That's what makes them so memorable to me. That's what makes them miracle inspired. They were decisions that I considered to be important. They were decisions that I made as thoroughly and thoughtfully as any important decision I have ever made. However, they were decisions that I changed because of some late presenting or oddly timed fact or event. They were decisions where the change surprised me, some I even regretted. But I never went back on the decision. I executed on those decisions with the same conviction that I have executed on every other decision that I deemed important in my life. I warned you in chapter 1 that each of my miracle-inspired decisions would appear inconsequential on their own, even boring. But in the context of my personal decision-making style, they are each profound. As they link together into my life path, they are miraculous. The third miracle-inspired decision that I can remember fits exactly the same pattern as the first two. It is this third miracle-inspired decision that I will describe in this chapter.

The year was 2001, and I needed to decide where I would go to work as my career at Arthur Andersen came to its unfortunate and unexpected end. This decision was not necessarily inspired. Gail was now the Global Managing Partner for BC. I had a leadership position in the northeast region. We had an opportunity to move over seven thousand consultants to KPMG Consulting, later renamed BearingPoint. After an extended and intense negotiation with both BearingPoint and Arthur Andersen—masterminded and led largely by Gail—the deal was struck, and one Friday in early July 2001, all seven thousand of us resigned from Arthur Andersen; and that very next Monday, we were hired into BearingPoint.

Our first year at BearingPoint was a whirlwind. The partners and senior leaders from BC were focused on reestablishing their relationships with their loyal clients and beginning to sell them new services. There were orientations to attend, integration of five thousand US based professionals into new industry and product delivery teams, relationships to establish, and conflicts to resolve. I spent a large portion of my first year with a small group of practice leaders working to get our US-based transplanted consultants assigned and productive on existing and newly sold BearingPoint projects. It was rewarding, exhausting, and frustrating all at the same time. But it was successful. When that first year was completed, Gail tapped me on the shoulder, and we quickly concluded that it was time to figure out where my permanent position at BearingPoint would be. I was a reasonably successful healthcare consultant. Remember, I was *reasonably* successful. Not my best showing. The practice leadership from the other regions of BC had spent their first year at BearingPoint establishing their presence and securing their leadership roles in the healthcare practice. There was no meaningful role in that practice for a reasonably successful leader. So I was offered the practice leadership role over the health insurance practice. I knew the industry from my earlier consulting days in BC which were personally some of my most successful. I had some relationships with industry leaders, and BearingPoint had a few client projects spread across the country which were led by a small number of industry experts. It was a for-profit industry which was always my preference. Most importantly, there was not a list of other leadership roles available to me; so I accepted the role.

The personal challenges that would come along with this role became quickly apparent. A big portion of the practice involved work we performed for the US government, more specifically, the Center for Medicare and Medicaid services—or CMS, by far the largest health insurance payer in the country. That meant that I spent most of my week in Washington DC and became a weekly commuter on the Delta shuttle. Upon further analysis of the active projects, the vast majority of the work was project management, good paying for BearingPoint, valuable work to our clients, but not necessarily work that would allow me to resell those consulting professionals as the industry experts that I thought them to be. Also, due to the nature of these existing projects, there were not industry relevant "products," tools, or repeatable services that I could glean from these projects to create an industry strategy or tangible sales plan. Remember: that was the strategy that enabled me to start the healthcare practice when I learned how to provide Revenue Cycle Management services from the other regions within BC. In short, lots of work to do.

So we got started creating services. I leaned on the claims, membership and customer service qualification that I and the small handful of legacy BC professionals had acquired. We built sales collateral and flew around the country to visit existing clients and test the salability of our new product suite with any health insurance company that would listen. Within the next several months, I made at least three day-trips between New York and California, as well as multiple other trips south to Florida, to the Midwest, and to multiple other destinations, south and west. I was tired, the sales were modest, the team was just okay, and I was setting up for another "reasonably successful" component to my consulting career. On top of all of that, BearingPoint was a fine place to work, but it was not the same as the Arthur Andersen where I grew up, and I did not get the same personal reward from working hard in an effort to "sell and deliver quality services [and] create loyal clients."

As my second year at BearingPoint was nearing its end, I had decided that it was time for me to move on. Nobody had tapped me on the shoulder. Nobody was pushing me to work longer, try harder, or sell more. I always suspected that it was because of my long and loyal relationship with Gail that the leaders within BearingPoint had not yet begun applying some pressure. I assessed that I had some time before such pressures would likely be applied, but it was clear to me that I was not going to achieve my career goals in my current position; I had to move on.

Northwell was still my most loyal client. Bob was more than a client; he had become a confidante and was on the way to becoming a mentor. Northwell was the first of my clients to award me work once I had exited BC and was flashing my new BearingPoint business cards. The first project Bob awarded us once we arrived at BearingPoint was to build a small data warehouse for their revenue cycle. It allowed Northwell's revenue cycle leadership to access data regarding revenue and receivables just a couple of days after month end. Previously, they needed to wait weeks for this data. To this day, nearly two decades later, Northwell still uses that data warehouse; they call it BearingPoint!

During one of my visits to the Northwell offices, Bob asked me to stay behind after a meeting. "What's wrong? You don't seem happy." From his tone, it was clear that he knew he was right. I told him a little about my current situation and work-related struggles. "Would you like to join us here at Northwell? We have several positions open, including the CFO position at Staten Island University Hospital (SIUH) and a new leadership position of the Health System's revenue cycle operation."

I didn't think it wise to refuse the opportunity to learn more about any viable option, but I didn't think that I was interested. Become a CFO? Actually lead a revenue cycle operation comprised of hundreds of employees? I didn't know how to do either one of those jobs. Work for a not-for-profit? I didn't think so. I was honest with Bob and told him that I did not think either of those roles made sense for me. However, I would be willing to learn more. He seemed eager to get me into the recruiting process. And so the process began.

My first interview was for the CFO position. It was a short drive to SIUH from my home in Brooklyn which included a trip over the Verrazano Bridge. Were I to be awarded this position it would be the shortest commute I would have ever had. I met with Tony, the CEO of SIUH. Tony has become a friend since that interview, but on that day he was all business. The interview was fairly intense, at least that was my perception. Maybe because it was in fact intense, maybe because I knew I had no business interviewing for the position of CFO in a fairly large hospital, possibly because Tony had every intention of awarding the position to the person who was currently doing the job on an interim basis. Whatever the reason, the interview did not go well, and within a couple of weeks it was announced that the job was awarded to the interim CFO. I wasn't terribly surprised, but I was disappointed. I wasn't sure if I wanted the job, and I was fairly confident that I was not qualified to do the job, but I hated to lose. I still do. I guess it fits with my other personality traits: hardheaded, stubborn, and controlling. I lost.

Within days of the interview, I got a call from Bob. "Hi Frank, I am calling to let you know regarding the CFO role. Staten Island has decided to go in another direction." That was the way, in their polite speak, that Northwell told you that you lost. In another direction—I lost. I still was not happy about it, but I liked the terminology: they decided to "go in another direction." I tucked that one into one of my memory banks and continue to use that one to this day.

Bob continued, "Why don't you come back in and interview for the other position I told you about? Leadership over the Health System's revenue cycle." I was back to the Northwell headquarters in Great Neck, Long Island the following week. To my surprise, the entire interview schedule was comprised of a meeting with Bob. The discussion was casual and comfortable. Bob explained to me the structure of the current revenue cycle operation. It was rather decentralized, even dis-integrated. I wasn't terribly surprised as I had consulted for Bob in this area several times over the prior several years. Really, he was looking for someone to run the billing function, which contains only a portion of the hundreds of steps that make up the revenue cycle. The position would be responsible for approximately four hundred employees. It would have indirect responsibility for the rest of the revenue cycle activities. "Indirect." At Northwell, I later learned, indirect meant that you were expected to make it better, but it reported to someone else. The position would carry a vice president title. As Bob described it: "I will expect you to improve the performance of our revenue cycle. The insurance companies need to stop denying so many of our claims, and they need to stop underpaying us. They do not pay us the way they promise to in our contracts."

To my surprise, with hardly asking me a question and without a single meeting other than with Bob, he was offering me the position. He told me the compensation, which would be slightly more than half of what I was currently making. Read it again: slightly more than *half* of what I was making. I was a little stunned at the speed with which we had reached this point in the process. I was very underwhelmed with the compensation offer. Still, I had a lot to think about. Bob was a loyal client and a confidante. As we parted company, I was positive. Possibly a little too positive. I promised to get back to him shortly.

As I drove home, I thought through the opportunity. I knew nothing about running this type of operation. I would have direct responsibility for four hundred employees that actually had to get real work done—much different from consulting to loyal clients about *how* they should get *their* work done! I would have "indirect" responsibility for the work of (to my best, educated estimate) at least another six hundred or seven hundred employees. More work that actually had to get done by people that did not even report to me. Northwell was—wait for it—a not-for-profit.

At least when I consulted to not-for-profits, I worked at a for-profit company. I was able to be an entrepreneur. I could build my business. How could I possibly, actually join a not-for-profit? How could that possibly help me achieve my career objectives? No more sales. No more profits to manage. No more businesses to build. No more loyal clients to create. I was approaching the age of 40. Retire early? With nearly a 50 percent pay cut? After having already taken a small pay cut when I moved to BearingPoint less than two years earlier? After losing my investment in the Arthur Andersen partnership? This was crazy! What about this interview process? I met nobody. Just Bob. Why didn't he want me to meet the CEO or the COO? What about the VPs who ran the other parts of the revenue cycle, the ones for which I would have "indirect" responsibility? Why wasn't I meeting any of them? In my typical decision-making style, I had thought through this and more factors during my approximately one-hour drive home. On the plus side, I had consulted to this revenue cycle over several years. I knew a number of the leaders. There was Bill and Caryl—God rest their souls—who had been running the billing office at Northwell for decades. There was Peggy; she helped us build the BearingPoint data warehouse which was a very successful project. There was Tina. Tina had joined Northwell about a year earlier. Before joining Northwell, she was a member of my healthcare group when we were at BC and was one of the 5,000 professionals that moved to BearingPoint. She was very talented, and I trusted her deeply. There was Patti. I didn't know her personally, but she had also recently joined Northwell. She was known across the industry as a revenue cycle expert. This was a pretty good team. I could work with them; but that was it. No other items on the plus side of the ledger. As I arrived home and pulled into the driveway, I had concluded that this was not the right job for me. I would stay at BearingPoint and keep looking. I still had some time, nobody was applying pressure for my *reasonable* performance as leader of the health insurance industry practice. Yes, I would stay at BearingPoint as long as April shared my opinions and didn't bring anything up that I had missed.

I spoke with April that very night. April is an interesting partner when it is time to make a big decision. Her and my careers progressed on very different paths. She was in real estate when I met her. As a matter of fact, I met her when I became a client of hers, looking for an investment property. I worked with her for a couple of months. She was good at what she did, but I was more interested in her than I was in the properties she showed me. That was not entirely my fault. I found April to be very attractive, beautiful, and so did my father who came on most of my real estate viewings. I think he was more anxious for me to date April than I was; he actually arranged for us to go on our first date during one of the viewings. The rest, as they say, was history. April worked for a mortgage broker after we got married and chose to become a stay-at-home mom when Christina was born. It was not until Madeline graduated college that she returned to the workforce as a medical records coder. April approaches questions and challenges from a completely different angle than I do. In fact, on occasions when we argue, it is most often because we have a decision to make, and our approach to the problem or question is so different that we confuse and frustrate each other. Sometimes we wonder if we are addressing the same question, but we always work our way through; and we always end up with a better, more informed decision because our approaches to the question are so very different.

So that very night, I shared my thought process on the possibility of joining Northwell. We talked for a while, and April concluded the same thing I did during my drive home. She assured me that she would support me in any decision I made, but it made no more sense to her than it did to me for me to accept the VP Revenue Cycle role at Northwell. So by the time we were done eating dinner, on the same day I had my interview with Bob, which was just a couple of weeks after my interview at SIUH and only a few weeks after Bob had first suggested that I consider a role at Northwell, I had decided that Northwell was not the right next step for my career.

With sweaty palms and butterflies in my stomach, I called Bob the next day. I didn't want to turn him down; I didn't want to tell him that I had "decided to go in another direction." But delaying it would only make the call that much harder to place. Bob was clearly surprised and disappointed. He thought I was going to take the job. I, in fact, was a little too positive when we finished up the interview because he actually thought I had accepted the job. I still contend that I had not. I did not have the heart or the stomach to take him through my and April's entire thought process. So I kept it simple. "I don't think that I am the right guy to run a revenue cycle operation or to have indirect responsibility for what is probably more than 500 people. I also cannot afford to take a 50 percent pay cut. I appreciate the offer, Bob, but I cannot join Northwell." As we hung up the phone, I sensed that I had done some damage to a relationship that I very much cherished, but I believed we would recover.

A few days later, the phone rang. It was Bob. He explained to me that he had discussed my candidacy for the VP Revenue Cycle role with his CEO, Michael. "Michael said that sometimes you have to pay a little more to get the talent you need into the organization. I am prepared to increase your offer." After doing some quick math, I determined that the new compensation offer would result in a pay cut of approximately 25 percent. That was far better than the original offer. Twenty-five percent. That's still a big reduction. That was it. He did not address my ability to run the revenue cycle operation. He did not address my concerns about the "indirect" responsibilities that I would need to manage. Naturally, he did not address my worries about joining a not-for-profit, my inability to create loyal customers, my inability to be an entrepreneur, my inability to build a business and manage profits—he couldn't address any of that because I had not even told him about all of that. As Bob gave his best effort to sell me on the new compensation offer, my mind began to wander. "Maybe it would not be so bad if I did not have to sell projects any more…that's stressful work. I could cut up my frequent flyer cards… say goodbye to my colleagues on the Delta shuttle. Christina and Madeline are getting close to their teenage years…maybe it would be good if I were home more. Why am I thinking these things? Twenty-five percent…that's a big pay cut."

"Yes." I accepted the job. Right there and then. I didn't say that I needed to think about it; I just said yes. I didn't need to talk to April again; she said she would support whatever decision I made. What had I just done? In an apparent compulsive decision, I just accepted a job I was not sure I could do, in a not-for-profit health system where I could not build a business, create loyal clients, or manage profits for a 25 percent pay cut. I accepted this job because Bob reduced the pay cut from nearly 50 percent to 25 percent, because in a few moments where my mind wandered, I concluded that not having to sell projects anymore might be a good thing, and because I would not need to fly anymore…because April and the girls needed me home more. Where did that random thought come from? April and I had never even discussed it. When I hung up the phone, I was somewhat stunned. No buyer's remorse but stunned. I could not believe what I had just done, but I did it; and I would never look back. This was the third miracle-inspired decision that I can remember.

Fourteen years later, I could write that down 100 times, and I still cannot justify accepting a 25 percent pay cut. What I did not realize then—what I could not have realized—is that this miracle-inspired decision brought me one giant step closer to the place that would save my life. But I was still the guy who did not like hospitals and was fearful of being in the same room with doctors. I was on a new path, but there were still some big decisions ahead if I was going to be able to deal with the mental and physical challenges that my future health condition would present.

CHAPTER
5

LENOX HILL

W hat would you think about if I asked you to consider the most difficult transition you ever had to endure? A common answer, for those who have experienced it, is the transition from high school to college, which I understand is often considered to be the most difficult transition many people make throughout their lives. You might also think about the transition from your school years to your working years—getting your first job. Possibly it was your transition from living the single life to living with your wife, husband, or life partner. If we consider the question, I think we can all agree that there is one transition that stands out in our life that was most challenging, most difficult.

I would say without much hesitation that the most difficult transition I have ever made in my life was my career move from BearingPoint to Northwell. I already explained that I was not sure that I was qualified to lead a group that was accountable for actually getting work done, as opposed to consulting to my clients on how they could or should get *their* work done; but that was only a small part of the difficult transition. In fact, it proved to not be much of a challenge at all. What made my transition so challenging was the complete change in mind-set that needed to occur as I moved from a profit-motivated organization to a mission-driven organization. Yes, I mean a not-for-profit.

Now, before I explain further, let me make it clear that I have developed quite a number of relationships with colleagues at Northwell that I value very much. I have met many smart, talented, and motivated people at Northwell. The vast majority of people I have met at Northwell are dedicated and very hard working. The mind-set is just so very different. The pace is different. The measures of success are different. The level of accountability for decisions and outcomes is different. It is all so very, very different.

Success in the profit motivated companies at which I worked was defined by three components: were your clients satisfied enough with your work to pay the bill, did you enhance your company's reputation in the market, or at least not diminish it, and did you make a profit? In a bit of an oversimplification, if you met those standards, you were successful. Of course, in such a competitive environment, you also had to be aggressive, be better than the person trying to do the same thing right next to you, be decisive, and get things done fast, effectively and efficiently. When profit is not the primary motivator, priorities change. More significantly to the impact on my transition, the pace changes. The view is longer term. The goal is to get it right for the beneficiary of the mission—in our case the patient—not to create a profit. There is clearly nothing wrong at all with a mission-focused mind-set, but when your role is not primarily patient facing, as mine was not, then time seems to slow down. My traditional measures of success were no longer valid. Defining and measuring return on the investments of our time, expenses, and capital expenditures were no longer paramount. Times have changed in the healthcare industry since 2004 when I joined Northwell and profit-focused measures of success are becoming more prevalent. However, the contrasts still exist. My entire approach to work, how I interacted with my colleagues, and my definition of success all had to change. It was a challenging transition, one for which it took years for me to become comfortable. I still do not think I have fully transitioned. Frankly, deep down, I do not even believe that I fit in this organization. I don't think I have fully adapted my mind-set. I don't think I have the patience. I don't think my way of thinking and the conclusions that I reach are fully understood or particularly valued.

Perhaps an early experience will help you understand more clearly what I am trying to describe. I joined Northwell the Tuesday after Labor Day, 2004. I was eager to get started. I understood my objective: reduce the frequency with which insurance companies fail to pay Northwell for the services we provide to our patients. I had a ton of ideas and many places I wanted to visit to learn more about how we did business. I had technologies I wanted to implement and consultants I wanted to hire to change organization structures and business processes. In one of my early meetings with Bob, he shared some advice with me. Actually, in his unique and fatherly style, he told me what I was going to do and how I was going to do it without making me feel deflated. "I want you to spend the next six months doing nothing." That's right, nothing. I was to meet as many people as I could across the hospitals, attend as many meetings as I was able to get myself invited to, listen, and learn. For the first three months I could ask questions. During the subsequent three months, I could offer opinions and even a possible suggestion. That was it; no more than that. In my previous jobs, I would have been terminated at my three-month probationary review. That is not an exaggeration; I had seen it happen to others. I grew up in a world where success meant you came up with the right answer, you made positive things happen fast, and you made it look easy. I honestly did not know if I could pull this off. I did not know if I had it in me to see things I thought should be changed and not ask for the change to be made immediately. It turned out that it was the best advice—or directive—that Bob could ever have given me. I learned a lot about the organization and the people in it. Politics were no more relevant here than they were where I had come from, but they were different. They were more personal. They were more emotional. I needed to understand that before I would be accepted into what was a terrific organization but was as much a club as it was a company. Some people who tried to teach me about the culture referred to it as a family, a reference which helped explain the nature of the politics but one with which I could never relate. Once again, as with my other miracle-inspired decisions, I never looked back—I never looked to change my decision or alter my course. I continued down the path.

Once settled in, I got to work on my objective. It was a project that consumed the majority of my time for the first three years at Northwell. It worked. Together with some of the revenue cycle leaders who were able to understand the vision, we recruited some new talent, brought in some new technologies, and completely changed the way we processed claims from the front of the revenue cycle to the back. Slowly and methodically, we standardized operations and centralized functions that were, understandably, relegated to second and third priority in the hectic hospital environment—an environment where the care of the patient always had to take first priority. We worked closely with those areas for which I was "indirectly" responsible, convincing them to adopt new ways of doing business and slowly bringing the most important revenue cycle functions under direct control. The strategy was effective. Within the first couple of years, we had improved cash collections and reduced dramatically the frequency with which insurance companies refused to pay for our services. What I could not realize at that point, around 2007, is that I had not nearly achieved the real purpose for which my path brought me to Northwell. I still was uncomfortable being in the same room with doctors, and I still did not like to be on the inside of hospitals.

I had been at Northwell for about three years when I was asked to consider a broader role. Northwell employs a fairly large group of physicians. In 2007, the group probably numbered near two thousand. As I write these words, they number near five thousand. The revenue cycle that performed billing and collection work for this growing medical group was in need of the same kind of improvements that we had just completed for the hospitals.

The Northwell organization structure is both vague and complex; we refer to it as "matrixed." The matrix necessitated that at least three executives approve of my appointment to this expanded role: Bob; Mark, the corporate COO; and Dennis, the Executive Director of the medical group. After a combination of individual and group discussion, it was determined that I would be assigned this expanded role. It was in this role that I met Felix, the capable and experienced leader of the medical group revenue cycle. Like so many of the professionals that I met at Northwell, Felix became a trusted colleague and good friend. We worked together intently over the following two years in an effort to replicate the success that Patti, Tina, Peggy, and the rest of the team in the hospital operation had achieved: improve the performance of the medical group revenue cycle, increase cash collections, and significantly reduce the frequency with which insurance companies failed to pay for the services we provided to our patients. This project, however, would be very different.

In the hospital operation, there were sixteen hospitals, each with one executive director at the helm. Secure their confidence, and changes flow rather smoothly. Sure, there are dozens of leaders and middle managers who needed to accept your proposed changes, but executive leadership was well-defined and of limited number. In the medical group, things are very different. There are sixteen service lines or specialties: Cardiology, cardiac surgery, neurology, neurosurgery, medicine, emergency medicine, urology, and so on. However, there were also two thousand doctors, and one of their names appeared on each of the literally millions of claims that were produced by the revenue cycle each year. Even more significant, the performance of the revenue cycle could directly impact the personal compensation of a number of those doctors. So the revenue cycle really had nearly two thousand masters. Each had their own unique personality; each had their own perspective on how the revenue cycle should work; and each was a doctor. Did I tell you yet how I felt about doctors? I needed a strategy and a way to overcome what I considered to be a personal problem.

My strategy was simple: create a plan for revenue cycle improvement—it would be very similar to the "centralize and standardize" strategy that I employed successfully with the hospitals; get to know the physician leaders of the largest and most politically powerful service lines; work to earn their respect and trust; and make some changes that would increase cash collections. If it worked, repeat. Cash is king in this industry, and success begets success. I worked feverishly for the next year with Felix and his leadership team. That work included meeting and sharing our plan with a number of the physician leaders. To be clear, this was anything but a smooth road. The most influential of the physician leaders thought my strategy was flawed, and that decentralization and service line ownership of these functions was the right path to improved performance. Many of the physicians aggressively asserted that the unique billing characteristics of their specialty could not be understood, preserved and further developed in our new centralized model. Still others wanted to know how we would—among the millions of bills produced per year—monitor each and every patient they cared for to assure accurate and timely payment. Yes, there were many challenges. There were many interests to be served. Bob, Mark, and particularly, Dennis had relatively low tolerance for unhappy physicians—understandably. The medical group was growing, and continuing to centralize administrative work was a fundamental component of the growth strategy. If successful, revenue cycle would become the poster child for centralization; if not, it would become the reason why the doctors would have no part of the concept of centralization going forward.

It was a challenging couple of years, but things worked out well. Physician leadership became willing to give the new model a chance, and we were all pleased when changes resulted in improved cash collections. Many of the physicians—not nearly all of them, but enough of them—recognized the improvement and became supporters, some vocal and some quiet. Quiet support is a big plus when the alternative could be hundreds of physicians complaining about problems with their collections. As 2008 came to a close, the revenue cycle had been improved, there was consensus about the improvement, and Bob, Mark, and Dennis were all satisfied with the progress. For sure, there was plenty more that could, and would be done, but the operation was in a good place and well-positioned for continued improvement.

I had personally achieved something else—something that seemed at the time to be just a pleasant side effect—but later, it proved to be much more important. I came to learn how to work with physicians. I also became increasingly comfortable working with them. For sure, I still thought that they made decisions differently than I did; they thought differently than I did. To this day I need to work a little harder when I am solving a problem with a physician. Nothing is a given; nothing can be assumed to be logical because our paradigms of logic are different. How could they not be? I was collecting cash; they were saving lives. The perspective is quite different, but it didn't matter anymore. I was comfortable being in the same room with my physician colleagues. I was comfortable working with them, making decisions with them. It was a big personal achievement. It was a personal achievement that would prove invaluable to my professional development and to my personal journey. I still, however, did not like being on the inside of hospitals.

I had established myself as a revenue cycle expert, both within and outside the walls of Northwell. This was a good reputation to have in an industry that was becoming increasingly cash-strapped and where insurance companies were becoming increasingly stingy with their funds. I was responsible for a growing hospital and medical group revenue cycle. Those responsibilities reached directly and indirectly to well over two thousand staff. I was figuring out the art of indirect leadership and influence. This was probably my most successful career run since my days in consulting when health insurers were consolidating and integrating. Just as things were working out so well, I got another tap on the shoulder. This one came out of the blue.

It was over a decade since the Health System had formed through the merger of two fierce competitors: North Shore University Hospital (NSUH) and Long Island Jewish Medical Center (LIJMC). For more than a decade, there was an intent focus on the centralization of non-clinical services. Purchasing, accounts payable, revenue cycle, payroll, and finance were among the functions that were centralized to create more effective and less expensive services. By 2009, Bob and Mark had concluded that there was too much finance pulled out of the hospitals. In fact, almost all of finance was centralized and the executive directors, none of which at the time had finance backgrounds, needed a partner in their operations to help them think through the initiatives and changes they were contemplating—a partner that could bring a financial perspective. The executive directors needed a strategic finance presence in their facilities, and Mark and Bob wanted me to create the prototype. I was asked to turn over the day-to-day operation of the revenue cycle to Patti and Felix so that I could spend the majority of my time as the CFO of the two largest hospitals, NSUH and LIJMC. The role came to be called CFO of the tertiary facilities (tertiary being a term used to refer to those hospitals that provide more complex services than a smaller community hospital). I accepted the role and started another new chapter in my career at Northwell.

The executive director at LIJMC was Chantel, and the executive director at NSUH was Susan. They were both terrific leaders and great partners to work with. There are plenty of great stories I can tell about both of them. I will focus for a while on my time at NSUH working with Susan as these experiences are the ones that furthered my journey down my personal life path.

Susan was a confident and capable hospital leader. A nurse by training, she spent much of her career working in cardiology and then with the chairman of cardiac services to build the operations that would become one of the largest and acclaimed interventional cardiology programs in the region. I first met Susan when I was doing work to establish charges for our hospital services. I had met with Susan multiple times during that process. She was cordial but guarded, even protective. Protective of the cardiac services for which she was responsible. She was no-nonsense. She showed up for meetings right on time, not a minute early, unless she was in a meeting with Dr. Stan, her chairman, in which case she was unapologetically late. She engaged in limited small talk, got right to business. She was open to almost any discussion or recommendation, but she was very knowledgeable about her service line. So if you wanted that discussion to remain cordial and for her to remain open to your recommendation, you had better have known what you were talking about. I respected her. She made my approach to setting charges more strategic, and I made her charges more relevant. So I was pleased that she was to become my boss at NSUH, and I think she was equally pleased that I would be her strategic finance partner.

Susan had a very strong team. They were capable leaders and were always looking at ways they could improve the hospital and our service to its patients. I became involved in all sorts of initiatives.

There were projects to improve the timing of services we delivered to our patients that would potentially shorten the amount of time they needed to spend in the hospital. Would they work? Did they work? There were projects to create new hospital units that would more rapidly assess patients who came to us with any variety of physical complaints, getting them out of the emergency department and determining more quickly if the patient needed to be admitted to the hospital or could go home. Would they work? Did they work? Did they affect overall revenue? Expenses? There were new patient services being evaluated and old ones that might be best if they were terminated. Should we? What was the result of these decisions? These were interesting projects, and I learned a lot about how hospitals work. I probably learned more during my time in that CFO role than I had learned in over a decade. But there was more about the time I spent at NSUH—experiences that would have a profound impact on my personal journey.

Susan was an operator. She wanted to know how things worked, and she knew you had to get into the details of the operation to truly understand. She referred to it as "natural curiosity," and you had to get "into the weeds" to understand how things worked. She thrived on it and respected others who did likewise. She believed that I had natural curiosity, and it was true that I could dive into the weeds as well as anyone. We worked well together.

NSUH is a large and complex facility, comprised of multiple buildings which were constructed over many years. This complex of buildings has been connected together as effectively, I assume, as its designers and architects could have hoped given it's Lego-like construction over decades of growth and development. Susan knew every inch of this vast complex. She even had mapped out a route through the building that would enable her to visit every unit in under four hours for her ceremonial Christmas morning rounds. She enjoyed connecting with the staff, and she very much enjoyed walking the building. She invited me to walk with her often. In the beginning, I would find any excuse possible to skip the walk. Hospital units, after all, were not my favorite places to visit, and I could be effective at my work with limited trips through the hospital. Susan was persistent. More and more she got me out of my office and onto the units. I mostly used this time on the units to meet staff and chat with physicians I had met and gotten to know since joining Northwell. For the longest time, I was able to avoid any meaningful contact with patients, and I stayed completely away from any of the procedural areas: the operating rooms, the cardiac catheterization labs, the endoscopy suites. These were the areas that made me most uncomfortable when it came to being inside a hospital. Susan became a mentor, a valued source of input, advice, and knowledge. She was my boss, but I think in some ways, I became a similar source of input and advice to her. She will be a mentor and friend for life.

In the couple of years or so that we worked together, we had numerous discussions about career development and our respective futures. Susan knew that I liked what I was doing in my relatively new role, but she could also tell that something was missing. She was right. As much as I liked what I was doing and found it rewarding, I no longer ran an operation. Funny, but the very thing that I was not sure I could do when I joined Northwell was now the thing that I wanted back; I wanted to run an operation again. During one of my discussions with Bob and also with Mark, I let them both know that I would like to be considered for a role somewhere in operations. I am pretty sure that Susan did the same for me.

Our routine tours through the hospital buildings became more frequent. Susan made it her business to expose me to as much of the operation as she could. I learned about capital allocation decisions. I became exposed to the hospital's clinical quality process—the protocols utilized to assess and assure that our clinical services are of the highest quality and the remediation processes we put in place to improve those services when it was found that they were not. Our tours through the hospital became more intense. She introduced me to the world of environmental services—all we do to keep every corner of the hospital sanitary, the sheets clean, and the units looking fresh. I learned about facility maintenance, how to staff a nursing unit, and food services.

One day we were touring a surgical unit, the collection of hospital rooms where patients are assigned to recover from any variety of surgical procedures. I greeted the nurses, inspected the floors and visitor space for cleanliness, and listened in on a group of clinicians discussing care strategies called the huddle. As we walked down the hall, I caught the eye of a male patient who was sitting in his chair in his semiprivate room. I paused for a minute, wondering if he would look the other way so I could walk off; but he didn't. Instead, our eyes locked in on each other, and I had no choice; from my position in the hallway at least fifteen feet away from the patient, I said hello. He smiled and said hello back. I edged my way to his door and asked him how he was feeling. He said he was feeling well today. He was holding a book of photographs, and he motioned for me to come into his room. Of course, I did (what choice did I have now), and he proceeded to show me some of the pictures in his book. He told me a little about his family. We chatted about his visit with us, the weather, what we each did for a living, and when he expected to go home. It was a perfectly lovely encounter. When we were done, I wished him well, shook his hand, and with a mutually exchanged smile, I left. I am not sure who benefited more from that visit. I think I needed it more than he did. When I left the room, I was met with a big smile from Susan. "That was the first time I ever saw you talk to a patient." It was the first time I ever had. "I think you are going to be good at this." I remember thinking that she could be right. I was no longer afraid of being in a hospital. I was comfortable. I could greet nurses, engage with doctors, and converse with patients—total strangers who were in a most vulnerable condition. Again, I was not aware of how important this development would be for me personally, but my whole perspective about hospitals had been changed. I owe that to Susan.

In 2010, Northwell acquired Lenox Hill Hospital (LHH). LHH was a tertiary hospital on the upper east side of Manhattan. It had a long and proud 150-plus-year history with a long list of clinical firsts and a legacy of hosting some of the highest regarded physicians in the region—and the country—in orthopedics, cardiac surgery, and other important specialties. But LHH had fallen on tough times. They were a stand-alone hospital in an era where consolidation of hospitals into health systems brought scale and relative stability. They were cash starved and had fallen somewhat behind in capital and clinical investment. Joining a system like Northwell was the best way to assure the LHH board that the hospital would be able to continue to service the upper east side community; and acquiring LHH was Northwell's opportunity to enter the prestigious Manhattan marketplace. It was a win-win opportunity, and by May 2010 it was a done deal.

It was late 2010 when I got a call from Mark. He had hinted at this several times in the past. Yet he had never asked the question. I was not surprised by the question, but a lot of time had passed since he had mentioned it last; I thought it might not happen. He wanted to know if I was ready and willing to travel into Manhattan and assume the position as executive director of Lenox Hill. I said yes. He instructed me to start working from Lenox Hill that very next Monday. The formal appointment would follow shortly. In that short discussion, I had made my fourth miracle-inspired decision.

This miracle-inspired decision was different than the first three. This was not a last-minute decision based upon an oddly timed event or thought or circumstance nor was it in conflict with my better judgment, my analysis of the situation, or my plan. I was not caught off guard by the question. No, this was not like my decision to join Arthur Andersen; it was not similar at all to the time that Eric appeared in my office doorway, or when Bob called me with an updated job offer and I said "yes" after my thorough, albeit speedy, analysis said absolutely "no." This was a relatively logical and uneventful "yes." What was miraculous about this decision was the uncanny setup. A few years earlier I would have never been able to accept such a position. Me? Work in a hospital every day? Alongside doctors? Not possible. Not possible until I spent time in the medical group revenue cycle working with doctors, until I met Susan who pushed and pushed until I agreed to round with her, until I made eye contact with a random patient in a random room and realized that I had it within me to have a positive interaction with a total stranger who, for a short period of time, was living in our hospital. Yes, this was every bit as much a miracle-inspired decision, not because of an unexpected and last-minute manipulation of time and events, but because of what I have come to realize was a very deliberate manipulation of opportunities, relationships, and work-related responsibilities that prepared me to say "yes," a manipulation that occurred over a three-to-four-year period. A manipulation that helped me overcome multiple personal obstacles that were far too significant to be labeled coincidences.

I have now described to you four of the six miracle-inspired decisions. The first miracle-inspired decision I described to you occurred when I was twenty-one. The fourth when I was forty-seven. Over that twenty-six-year period, these four miracle-inspired decisions created a path that took me from staff accountant in a Big 8 accounting firm to the executive director of Lenox Hill Hospital. Still, my preparation was not complete; and I have not yet described to you how I so greatly benefited for this lifetime of preparation. It is in the chapters that follow where I attempt to describe these last important steps on the path that has been my life.

CHAPTER 6

REVELATION

I worked at Lenox Hill for just over two years. That included a leave of absence that lasted four months. I will tell you more about the events surrounding that leave of absence later. In this chapter, I will share how my time at Lenox Hill completed my preparation for my most difficult life challenge in a most remarkable fashion.

Running a hospital was about the most challenging career experience of my life. It is wildly different than anything else I have ever done. When you spend day after day in a hospital, you come to truly realize and appreciate the impact that clinical professionals have on the lives of their patients and their families. These clinicians save lives every day. We all know that; that's what happens in a hospital, right? It is astounding, however, to actually see it happen every day. It is awesome to know and watch surgeons come into the hospital and practice their trade in the operating room, invading human bodies, removing or repairing organs, and sending those patients home in better condition than they were when they arrived hours or days before. You can see it every day. These patients and their families are vulnerable, scared, relying on these clinical experts to save and extend their lives, the lives of their loved ones. These clinical experts don't just fix these broken bodies. They tend to their fragile emotions. They tend to their fears. They care for their minds as well as their bodies. Hospitals are amazing places, and having the privilege to observe one perform day after day is incredible. Notice I said "observe." Yes, I was the executive director. I was "in charge." But a hospital is not just a place. It is a complex and dynamic organism. Such an entity cannot be "managed." It can be guided, it can be supported, it can even be challenged to achieve better things tomorrow than it did today; but a hospital is comprised of doctors and surgeons, nurses and social workers, kitchen staff and environmental workers, and construction workers and maintenance staff. It is a small self-sufficient city that takes care of every need of its temporary residents. It contains thousands of dedicated staff with a broader array of skills and competencies than any single leader can comprehend. Manage? I don't think so.

There is another dimension to hospital life that we all know but is incredible to witness. There are no locks on the front door of a hospital. They never close. They are open every weekend, every holiday, even days that government and commercial buildings are closed due to weather or natural disaster. Even when there are no visitors, hospitals are caring for their temporary residents—their patients—every hour of every day of every week of every year. Lenox Hill was open for business during Hurricane Katrina when so many buildings, even some hospitals, were evacuated due to extensive flooding. So the days were long, and I was on call every night and every weekend.

Surgeons start their first cases in the operating room around 7:00 a.m. Some of them liked to stop by my office before their first case. Sometimes to say hello, sometimes to complain about something that happened the day before, sometimes just to make sure that I knew they were operating that day. There was no need to let me know that. I knew the schedule every day. I knew who was operating and the procedures they were performing. The operating rooms are the epicenter of the facility. What happens in these procedure rooms defines a hospital's reputation in the marketplace and is directly tied to a hospital's ability to achieve its financial targets.

Some surgeons liked to come by after their last case. That often occurred around 5:00 or 6:00 p.m. I came to understand the rhythm of the place. I knew who operated on Mondays, who operated on

Thursdays. I knew who would stop in on Tuesdays at 6:45 a.m. and who expected I would be available to see them on Thursday at 5:30 p.m. Workdays were long, and evenings and weekends were occasionally interrupted with emergency calls. Calls when computer systems went down. Calls when unexpected events occurred that might affect patients. Calls when celebrities were in the hospital. Calls.

I enjoyed all aspects of my work at Lenox Hill. The thing I enjoyed more than anything, however, was walking the building. I should really say buildings. Like many hospitals, Lenox Hill was a complex of 10 buildings, each constructed at different times over its 150-plus-year history. Like NSUH, these buildings were interconnected to appear to its inhabitants to be as close to a single structure as its designers and architects were able to make it. Susan's lessons lived inside of me, and I walked the building as often as I could make the time. I often walked with Gus, the hospital's CFO. He was assigned to Lenox Hill nearly a year before I was, and he always knew the facility and the people even better than I ever did. We would walk the maternity ward, the nursery, and the neonatal intensive care unit. We walked the surgical units where patients recovered from any variety of surgical procedures, and we walked the medicine units where patients were being treated for any variety of chronic or acute conditions that did not require surgery. We have a separate orthopedics floor, which was usually filled to capacity with patients who had just received a new hip or knee. Ironically, I enjoyed walking all of these units, talking to the nursing staff and greeting patients.

For the better part of the first year that I was there, I avoided visiting one place: the operating rooms, or as we called them, the ORs. The ORs were never part of my routine rounding with Susan, and I was still not sure that I could meet patients just before or after this most stressful event in their lives. I was still not a fan of seeing blood, and I would be the laughing stock of the hospital if I repeated my embarrassing episode when I went to visit Domenick after he had his appendix removed; this time in front of the doctors and nurses who lived in this environment every day. So I avoided this space that I still dreaded, which occupied real estate within the walls of the place that I was beginning to think of as my second home. I knew that I could not avoid it forever. I didn't want to. As I have said before, the ORs are the epicenter of the hospital. Could a contractor be effective if he never visited his construction sites? Could an auto industry executive be a credible leader if she never visited the factory floor? The doctors expected me to show up at some point to show my interest in what they did. I had a responsibility to make it known that I cared about the people in the ORs, that the staff were treated with respect by the surgeons, and that the patients were the beneficiaries of all of our safety practices and protocols.

Deb was the head nurse responsible for OR operations. She and her team of nurses made sure that each OR was set up and ready for the doctor and the procedure that was to be performed next. They assured that protocol was followed when the ORs were cleaned between procedures, and that safety procedures, called time-outs, were properly executed before each surgery. The time-out was a so called "best practice" adopted from the airline industry where the entire crew comes together before the flight begins to go over every aspect of the trip, from destination to passenger list to equipment checklists. In the time-out, every member of the team has the right and responsibility to speak their mind about anything they see or don't see that might be a risk to a successful flight, regardless of their rank, years of experience, or place in the pecking order within the flight crew. Time-outs have helped the airline industry avoid many mishaps in the air, and they have helped the hospital industry avoid many errors in the OR. Deb and her team were also responsible for making sure procedures got started on time, especially the first pro-cedure of the day in each OR, and they were responsible for assuring that each OR was staffed with the properly trained team of nurses to support the given surgery. It is an awesome responsibility in a theater that is busy and demanding, one where doctors commanded the utmost respect and demanded nothing short of perfection. It is a theater where mistakes impact lives—the lives of those people on the operating table and the lives of their loved ones seated patiently in the waiting room. Deb and I met often in my office. We reviewed the day's procedures, problems, and successes. She often asked me when I would tour the ORs with her, and I always told her that one of these days I would find the time.

At the end of one of our routine meetings, I turned to Deb and told her that it was time for me to spend a day with her in the ORs. We picked a date and agreed to meet in my office at 5:30 a.m. I was not looking forward to my day in the ORs. There was very little about this experience that I anticipated would be pleasant or even comfortable. Some of these patients would be in pain, or at least in some level of distress, no doubt worried about their pending surgery and recovery. I would encounter the families of these patients, equally concerned about the welfare of their loved ones. What would I say to one of these family members if my eye caught theirs like it did that day I was rounding with Susan? This would surely be a more difficult encounter. What would I do? How could I relate? Surely in this setting, nobody would be particularly interested in discussing the weather. What if I went pale and my lips turned white? I had every expectation that this would be a personally challenging day.

The night before we were to tour, Deb dropped off my OR scrubs, and by five-fifteen that next morning, I was in my scrubs and waiting for Deb to swing by my office so that we could walk to the ORs together. Deb showed up right on time and we walked together to the tenth floor. The entire tenth floor is dedicated to the surgical suite: reception and visitor waiting area, the patient prep area, twenty-two operating rooms, and the PACU, the post-acute care unit, where patients recovered for their first few hours after surgery. My tour tracked the same path a patient would take through the maze that was the tenth floor. I was nervous, but I did my best to look and act as I would on any other day: hiding my nerves from Deb and eventually from the doctors, nurses, patients, and family members I would encounter that day.

I should not have been, but I was immediately struck by the amount of activity taking place on the tenth floor, and it was not even 6:00 a.m. As we entered the visitor waiting area, there were already a number of family members settling in for the stressful vigil they were about to endure, a time that I imagined would feel to them like an eternity before they would see their loved one again. I saw in their faces concern, distress, even fear. My stomach became unsettled for the first time that early morning just from thinking for those short moments what these people were feeling, just from thinking what would soon happen to their loved ones. Deb and I were both in scrubs, and scrubs get attention when they walk through a hospital waiting area. Most of the visitors tracked us as we walked the pathway through the many seats to the reception desk. As we neared the end of that path, my eye connected with that of a middle-aged woman seated alone. I wanted to look away, but I just could not. I slowed my pace just a bit, and with a slight smile greeted her with a "good morning." With an appreciative expression on her face, she returned my greeting, and as I walked by, I told her, "I hope everything goes well for you today." With what seemed like a tear in her eye, her smile widened slightly. "Thank you." I only had a moment before we would pass the reception desk and enter the patient prep area, known as pre-op. In that moment, I thought to myself how that was not so bad. I said a quick silent prayer for the health of the patient for whom she was waiting and was quickly distracted by our entry into pre-op.

A lot happens in pre-op, and any novice to the hospital environment would have thought it was two o'clock in the afternoon, certainly not 6:00 a.m. Several patients had already changed into their hospital gowns and were seated in a lounge chair. Some were being interviewed by a nurse, some were receiving their hospital wrist bands, and some were just seated waiting for their next step in the process. They all looked nervous. Some looked pensive. Some looked downright afraid. The intensity of the activity was impressive. The nurses and staff knew that it was their job to assure these patients would be ready to meet with their doctor in the next few minutes. There were questions to be asked, instructions to be given, and medications to be administered. Within the next half hour, each patient would receive a visit from their OR nurse, anesthesiologist, and surgeon. Each would start with the same question: "Can you tell me your name and what you are here for today?" Being asked to identify themselves so many times was unnerving to some patients, but I knew that it was a basic element of patient safety, and as I walked through pre-op, I listened to hear if the staff was following this fundamental protocol.

Another element of safety occurs when the surgeon pays his or her visit. After the surgeon asks the "who are you and why are you here" question—which seems very odd to most patients as they have met their surgeon at least a few times by now—the surgeon places an "X" at the surgical site with a magic marker and initials the spot. He then asks the patient to explain the procedure they are about to receive and to confirm that the right spot has been marked. This requires the patient to confirm the surgical site and all but eliminates the occurrence of a wrong site surgery. Surgery on the wrong knee, for example, occurred more often across the country than most people would think before this simple safety procedure was adopted. I witnessed several surgical site markings during my visit to pre-op that morning. As time ticked by, the pace of activity continued to accelerate. By 7:00 a.m. as many as twenty-two patients will have been prepped and escorted to their assigned operating room. After a short respite for the nurses in pre-op, that process would begin again for the second, third, and sometimes fourth round of patients on any given day.

So far so good. It was well before 7:00 a.m. when Deb and I headed toward the ORs. There was plenty for Deb to check on before the first patient was escorted in. As we left pre-op, my stomach became unsettled for a second time. This time it lasted longer.

The tenth floor is a bit of a labyrinth, designed and built to contain as many ORs as possible, together with a sufficient amount of space allocated for pre-op and PACU to reduce the possibilities of any back-ups in the ORs. Naturally, hallways connect these patient care areas. These hallways wind behind and around the patient care spaces, and it can often seem that you are walking far more steps than the ground you are actually covering. As we walked from the pre-op to the ORs, that is exactly how it felt to me. Deb and I made several left and right turns as we walked. I was not particularly looking forward to our arrival in the ORs, so I can't say I minded that the walk took longer than I thought it would. We didn't talk much during this walk, and I thought that Deb was able to tell that I was becoming increasingly nervous. As we walked, I could not help but think how many patients walked this very hallway on their way to meeting their surgeon for their procedure. These procedures save lives, but that morning it felt like a long walk to the electric chair. How unnerving it must be to be a patient walking this walk.

That's right. As long as they are able, patients are given the option to walk themselves to the OR. I always thought this was a humane practice, which is followed in most hospitals. You see, during pre-op, it seems to me that the patient is quite literally stripped of their identity. They turn over their wallets, handbags, identification, money, and credit cards. The only form of identity they carry is the white band that was secured to their wrist in pre-op. They remove all jewelry, including items they might be used to wearing every day like their wedding ring or watch. They remove every stitch of clothing that is their own and are required to don a hospital gown that looks like every other gown on every other patient in the facility. They hand in their dentures and are instructed to wear no makeup. They look nothing like they normally do when they leave their homes. They follow the instructions of those caregivers around them, surrendering for a time their ability and instincts to use their own judgment to say yes or no. In my mind, they are, for a time, stripped of who they are. So allowing the patients to walk this walk on their own two feet seems to give them back some piece of their dignity, some small piece of control in a moment where they are in a place where they do not want to be, doing what they do not want to do, and looking like they do not want to look.

We were what turned out to be approximately halfway through our walk to the ORs when we passed the only set of windows in the entire hallway. I looked out at a view of several random Manhattan buildings. The sun was coming up, and it looked like it was going to be a clear and bright day. I thought in that moment how cruel it was that our patients could catch a glimpse of the outside, reminded of the freedoms so many millions of New Yorkers were enjoying at that very moment that they were about to climb onto their assigned operating room table.

At the end of what seemed was going to be this endless hallway, we reached the entrance to the ORs. We were about to enter a sterile area, and the signs made it clear that appropriate scrubs, booties, headwear, and masks were required. With all the appropriate gear in place, we entered. There were no patients in any of the ORs yet. All the surgeons were most likely in pre-op greeting and autographing their patients. Yet the ORs were an absolute flurry of activity. Every OR was assigned a nurse, and each of them was diligently working to assure that every detail was exactly right before their patient and surgeon arrived. There was equipment to assure was in place and instrument trays to confirm were complete and correct for the particular procedure and surgeon. Supplies needed to be counted and checked, and the presence of the necessary implants—artificial knees or hips, for example—needed to be confirmed. There were dozens of details to tend to, and 7:00 was coming fast. We visited each of the twenty-two operating rooms, and many of the nurses had last-minute questions for Deb. She handled them all effectively and professionally.

As 7:00 approached, the hallways between the operating rooms became eerily quiet. The frenetic pace of activity seemed to slow almost to a halt. That's only how it appeared on the outside of the ORs. The players had entered their respective theaters. One by one, the patients were escorted down the sterile hallway and into their respective ORs. My stomach churned again as I saw the helpless expressions on so many of their faces. Shortly after the patients came, the anesthesiologists and the surgical teams arrived. Usually, the surgeon arrived last. Most of the patients arrived by 7:00. Deb and I moved in and out of several of the ORs as the surgical teams completed final preparations with their patients. I witnessed several time-out procedures. Last-minute questions were asked and answered. I observed in each OR that we visited that the surgeon was present and spoke to the patient one last time before the anesthesia was administered, another of the safety protocols I was there to observe.

By 7:45, most of the procedures for this first round of patients were underway. I thought for a moment that the pre-op area would start getting busy again, preparing the second round of patients for their walk down the hallway. In the meantime, I rounded the ORs with Deb as she made her routine quality visits to the now active ORs.

At one of our stops, we visited with Dr. Nirav, Lenox Hill's finest cardiac surgeon. He was still finalizing prep for the coronary artery bypass graft (CABG) he was about to perform. The CABG is a fascinating procedure. The surgeon must stop the patient's heart for a period of time. As a result, the patient is placed on a heart-lung machine which literally keeps the patient alive during the multiple-hour procedure. We had just acquired a new heart-lung machine for the hospital, and I spent my time in this OR seated with the technician behind the machine, observing its use and function. The machine is large and impressive. I remember seeing the patient's blood flow into the machine, circulating through, and then back out and into the patient. I was impressed to witness it operating and equally impressed with my own performance. I was actually inside an operating room during a procedure and watching a machine process a patient's blood, and I was surprisingly calm. I was becoming used to the OR environment. We moved on to the next OR slightly after Dr. Nirav began to work.

Our next stop was a visit with Dr. Peter who performs complex surgeries on cranial-based tumors. He also performs a variety of other procedures on the head, face, and neck. Dr. Peter had already become and remains a friend and confidant. It is interesting to come to know a person and then to observe them in their work environment, especially when the person is a surgeon and their work environment is the operating room. I always knew Dr. Peter had an excruciating attention to detail. It was always apparent in the way he ran his clinical practice, the way he dressed, and even the way he kept his office—impeccable. Inside the operating room he was a perfectionist. When I visited, he was in final preparations for the procedure he was about to perform. He inspected the room, the instruments, and the supplies in detail. Everything was not only in order, but the nurse that prepared the room clearly understood Dr. Peter's desire for everything to be perfectly placed and organized. He assessed all aspects of his work area and every supply and piece of equipment on the instrument table. His team respected him, and he respected his team. I spoke briefly to Dr. Peter before he started his procedure and remained briefly as he began his work. Again, I surprised myself as I was nearly unaffected by being present during a surgical procedure. My stomach did not become unsettled. I was not concerned that I would become pale or need the assistance of a nurse to keep from passing out. Deb and I continued our rounds.

We visited Dr. Jose, one of Lenox Hill's finest orthopedic surgeons. He was performing a knee replacement surgery. When we arrived, he had already prepared the knee and had fitted the new knee for placement. He was in the process of installing the new knee. It had been described to me that orthopedic surgeons were the carpenters of the surgical community. Seeing the placement of this knee, I now knew why. It is a rough process, not dissimilar from watching a woodworker installing a support beam that doesn't quite fit into its spot. Using his hammer and saw, that woodworker eventually convinces that beam to sit neatly into its space. If you can imagine that woodworker's effort, you have an idea of what I was watching. It was awesome to observe the team work together to complete such intricacies in a routine and collaborative manner. I must admit that I found it equally impressive that I was able to witness such a procedure. No problem. No unsettled stomach. I was not uncomfortable being inside the ORs. I was not in a hurry to leave. I was not dreading the rest of the day nor was I wishing that the day was over. I was becoming more at ease in what was to me a very unusual environment.

Deb and I spent the rest of the day rounding the ORs. I observed a number of additional safety protocols effectively executed as patients were escorted into their assigned operating rooms throughout the day. I also observed the ORs "turn," the process of cleaning, sterilizing, and resetting the OR in preparation for its next patient.

We toured the PACU where the same patients I met in pre-op were now recovering from their procedures. I saw their loved ones at their bedside, the same people that sat pensively in the waiting area just hours before. Both the patients and their loved ones looked calmer now, their worries relieved. They comforted each other and were comforted by their nurse and care team, whose job it was to monitor these patients and help to manage their pain in the minutes and hours right after their procedure. I saw empathy in this room. I saw compassion. I saw patients beginning to heal and their family members hopeful that their toughest days were behind them. I saw relief. I saw hope. I remembered my walk to the ORs hours earlier and how that walk seemed to me then to be like a walk to the electric chair. How could I have thought that? On the contrary, for our patients, that is a walk of hope—hope for a cure or for a repair or some form of healing that would make life normal again.

It had been a very long day, and I was very tired. At the same time, for me it was a day of revelation. My view of the operating room had changed. I did not know at the time how important that change would be for me on a very personal level.

FRIDAY THE THIRTEENTH

One doctor that was not operating that day when I visited the ORs with Deb was Dr. Mike. Dr. Mike is a urological surgeon who arrived at Lenox Hill some time before I did. Urological surgeons specialize in diseases of urinary organs, including the bladder, kidney, adrenal gland, and male reproductive organs. Dr. Mike is a highly competent surgeon, concentrating a significant amount of his work on complex cancer surgeries. He had been brought into Lenox Hill before the hospital became a part of Northwell Health, during a time when the hospital was in need of attracting some well-known physicians with impressive reputations. Dr. Mike attracted a large number of patients from within and outside the New York area with his reputation for high-quality outcomes and low complication rates. For Lenox Hill, he was the "rock star" in what was otherwise a relatively routine, even sleepy, urology service. Dr. Mike was highly motivated, extremely confident, and quite outspoken. His skills both in the operating room and at the bedside created devoted and very satisfied patients. His large number of complex surgeries, low complication rates, and virtually zero surgical errors contributed favorably to the financial performance of the hospital.

Like many of the physicians, Dr. Mike visited me frequently. Again, like his peers, he normally visited to complain about some negative experience he had somewhere in the hospital or to make sure I knew what he was doing or that he was operating that particular day. Dr. Mike, however, was a little different. He also came by to tell me what was going on in his specialty, what he saw or learned at a recent conference he had attended, and—most unique among the other doctors—exactly what he did and how he did it. I never really understood why he wanted me to understand his work to the extent that he explained it to me. On several occasions he brought video documentation of actual procedures he had performed. Much of his work was in the treatment of kidney cancer or renal cell carcinoma (RCC). These procedures often included a nephrectomy or the removal of the diseased kidney, and in the more complex cases, the removal or surgical treatment of other organs or tumors. It was with these more complex cases that Dr. Mike created his reputation and on which he presented and spoke at many conferences. It was the videos that he used at these conferences that Dr. Mike brought to my office and used to explain to me how he performed these surgeries. I had never heard of renal cell carcinoma before and within several months of starting at Lenox Hill I came to know more about its treatment than I ever thought I would want or need to know.

It was Friday, July 13, 2012. I am not particularly superstitious, but in light of the events that would begin on this Friday the thirteenth, I think it is interesting to mention. I was on a rare business trip to Chicago, returning to New York. I was to arrive in New York by 5:00, make a quick stop home, and April and I would hop into the car for the two-and-a-half-hour ride to our vacation home in Upstate New York. Now, this house upstate is the subject of another miracle-inspired decision that I will explain in a future chapter. For now, it is only relevant that, to this day, I enjoy my time upstate so much that I would be making the trip for this particular weekend just about an hour after my flight landed at Kennedy airport.

I arrived at O'Hare Airport in Chicago early that Friday afternoon. As is my routine, I stopped in the men's room before proceeding to the gate. To my surprise, I saw blood in my urine. This had never happened before. I knew that blood dissolves in other liquids and can look like more than it actually is, but this looked like an awful lot of blood to me. I don't know much clinically, but even then I knew that blood in the urine could be from kidney stones or from a bladder infection. A quick internet search confirmed that I was correct but that there are also a variety of other potential causes. I was, at least for the time, pleased that mine was accompanied by absolutely no pain. I decided not to worry about it. I had to get back to New York and was looking forward to a relaxing weekend upstate. Besides, I worked at a hospital. This would wait until Monday when I would have my choice of physicians with which I could consult.

My trip back to New York was uneventful, and our ride upstate was pleasant. I barely mentioned the episode to April, and we both concluded that on Monday I would likely learn that I had an infection or a stone to tend to. I remember hoping that it would not be a stone. I knew that those caused quite a bit of pain. Being a bit of a hypochondriac, I was concerned that I would experience some pain that might disrupt my weekend. It was the early hours of Saturday morning when we had finally settled in and were relaxing upstate. So far so good. No pain and no more blood. I was becoming confident that this would be nothing to worry about. Maybe I would not even need to consult with a doctor on Monday. For a while, maybe I would just see what happened.

I woke up the next morning with plans for an enjoyable day in the country. I felt great, but once again there was blood in my urine. Thankfully, still no pain. This time, April was able to see it, and we both agreed this needed some attention. We proceeded with our day's plans, but during our drive into the village I decided I should call a doctor, but who? I could call Dr. Carl, the chairman of the emergency department. These professionals jokingly referred to themselves as the jack-of-all-trades. That's because emergency medicine physicians are virtually the only doctors that are trained to assess and treat any variety of physical and mental conditions; a patient with literally anything wrong with them could walk into the emergency department, and the emergency medicine physician needs to be prepared to care for that patient. I could call Dr. Tony. Dr. Tony was a general surgeon by training who now served as the medical director of Lenox Hill. A valued member of my leadership team, Dr. Tony tended to all matters clinical in the hospital. He had taught me a lot during my short time at Lenox Hill, and I trusted him deeply. Surely, he could give me some good advice. I gave it some thought and pushed the hands-free button on the steering wheel. I said, "Call Dr. Mike." After all, he is a urologist. That's where I am going to eventually end up anyway. That is where I might as well start. Dr. Mike answered promptly, and after some collegial pleasantries, I explained to him what had transpired over the past two days. Dr. Mike had some questions, and I answered them in the same rapid-fire fashion as they were asked: "Yesterday was the first time that it happened," "It happened again this morning," "No, it never happened before yesterday," "Yes, I am sure." Then he asked me, "Do you have any pain?" I told him that I did not. The pregnant pause that followed irked me just a bit. He asked a few more question, and then once again, "Are you sure that you have no pain?" I went from irked to unsettled and assured him that I had none. We agreed that I would meet him in his office first thing Monday morning. He prescribed an antibiotic which I was to start that day, and for the first time, I was wishing that my weekend would get interrupted by a little pain. At this point, I was even willing to endure a lot of pain. It was clear that Dr. Mike would have felt better if I had told him that I was in pain.

The rest of the weekend went by pain free. April and I enjoyed dinner out on Saturday night, and we did a reasonably good job of not anticipating what bad news we might learn on Monday. I was in the hospital bright and early on Monday morning, and Dr. Mike was prepared to see me as soon as I called. It was convenient as his office was on the third floor of the hospital. My visit was brief: a few more questions, some vital signs, and some blood work. He ordered a CT scan of my abdomen, suggesting that I have it done at NYU Medical Center where he had a long-term relationship with the chair of radiology, whom Dr. Mike trusted very much. So I did. Before noon, I drove the short trip downtown and was registered in the department of radiology for my scan. Minutes later, I was wearing the first hospital gown I had ever donned (not as dreadful as I had at one time anticipated), and I was being slid into the CT scanner.

A CT scan is a relatively simple test to endure. You are slid into a donut-shaped device, slid back out, and that process is repeated a few times. During the ride, hundreds of X-ray images are taken by the machinery inside the donut. The result is a series of pictures of your insides in successive slices. Within a few minutes the test was complete, and I began a brisk walk to the men's locker room to get dressed back into my own clothes. Before I could disappear down the corridor, I heard a strange voice call, "Mr. Danza, Dr. Mike would like you to have a second scan. He would like us to scan your chest." The voice, as it turned out, came from the mouth of the chair of the department of radiology, who had obviously read my first scan as it was being completed. I was fairly certain that this could not possibly be good news, but to their credit, the department chair and all his staff involved in my first scan were completely unemotional; they were calm. I went back into the room where I had just completed my first scan, and a few minutes later, my second scan was complete. As I walked out of that room for the second time, I turned as if to walk toward that locker room, but I knew it was not to happen. It did not. As soon as I appeared out of the scanning room, I heard that same voice. "Mr. Danza, Dr. Mike is on the phone, and he would like to talk to you." Of course, I was now quite nervous. This would not be good. Still, I had no idea what he was going to tell me. Dr. Mike was on the speaker phone when I arrived in a small room at the far end of the department. I said hello, only to make sure he knew I was in the room. The department chair who had read my scan was in there with me. This time there were no pleasantries. The next words came from Dr. Mike: "Frank, you have cancer. Renal cell carcinoma, kidney cancer. It has metastasized to your lungs. You have multiple tumors in both lungs. It is stage four."

My reaction was calm, but it was irrational. "That's not possible. You must have made a mistake. I have been feeling good. I have been active, and I am full of energy. This can't be my scan." Dr. Mike's response was empathetic, but very direct. "There has been no error. Go home. Take a cab if you are not up to the drive. Call me when you are together with your wife, and I will fill you both in on this condition and what needs to happen next."

It did not strike me until sometime later, but what were the odds? What were the chances that I would accept a position, of all things, running a hospital, meet a highly skilled surgeon who specialized in complex RCC cases, learn about the disease and the surgery, and how this particular surgeon performed it—with videos—and then only a couple of months later contract this relatively rare disease? What were the chances? I have thought about it often and can only conclude that I was beginning to reap the rewards of those miracle-inspired decisions. That's right. Though this was one of the darker days of my life, where would I have been had I not become comfortable navigating hospitals and interacting with doctors? What if I had never met Dr. Mike? What would I have done then?

I didn't want to leave my car downtown, so I decided to drive myself home. To be honest, I don't remember anything about that drive. I don't remember the route I took. I don't remember if there was traffic or if the roads were clear. I don't even remember retrieving my car from the parking garage, paying the parking fee, or tipping the attendant. The next thing I remember after Dr. Mike told me to go home was putting my key into the lock in our kitchen door. April had not yet restarted here career after staying home to raise Christina and Madeline, and I saw her through the glass pane in the door. What in God's name was I going to say when I opened that door? April did not even know that I was coming home early, let alone the life-altering news I was about to deliver. I opened the door; April must have seen the look of desperation on my face because she came across the kitchen to me. I hugged her and started to cry. I couldn't say anything. I couldn't say IT. Finally, I said it through my whimpers: "I have cancer." It was the first time I said it, and it was one of the hardest things I had ever said. I would say it a dozen times or more after that before I was able to get the words out without a whimper, before I could say it and actually believe it. April had a similar reaction to mine. "You must mean that Dr. Mike thinks you might have cancer, and you need to have some tests." My response was as direct as Dr. Mike's. "The tests were done, and I have it—kidney cancer."

We comforted each other for a short time and then we got to work. In times of trouble, that is what April and I do best. We get stuff done. In many ways it is therapeutic. We called Dr. Mike on the speaker phone. Dr. Mike assessed my case for the both of us. "Frank has stage four kidney cancer. That means that the tumors had spread to his lungs. It may have spread to other parts of his body, but we'll worry about that after the surgery." Surgery…? Dr. Mike continued, "The main tumor has grown outside the bounds of Frank's kidney. It has grown up the vena cava, the vessel that carries blood from the lower half of the body back to the heart. The tumor is only inches from Frank's heart, and surgery is required immediately. A portion of the tumor could separate at any time and move to the heart, causing an immediate and fatal heart attack."

My miracle-inspired decisions to the rescue again. Had I not followed the life path I was on, I surely would have delayed my doctor's visit for at least some time, and with no knowledge of healthcare or relationships in the industry, it would have likely taken me weeks or more to select a doctor, get an appointment, and have a scan. Instead, that all happened in the course of two days. Either way, this was serious. I was to go back to Dr. Mike's office for pre-surgical testing (PST) the next morning, which was Tuesday, and I was scheduled for surgery first thing Wednesday morning.

When we hung up with Dr. Mike, our work was not done. I had to let them know at work what was going on, and somehow we needed to tell my family. I called Mark. The discussion was short and effective, with exactly the amount of caring and empathy you would hope for from your boss after sharing news that was as shocking to him as it was to my own wife. Mark asked who I wanted to run the hospital until I felt better. I immediately responded that it should be Gus. With that business behind us, he wished me well, and our discussion was ended. Next order of business: how would we tell the family. This was going to take its toll on my aging mother. A widow, she lived right across the street, and we were and still are very close. My two brothers and sister would be shocked. My nieces would want to know if I was okay. This was too much for me to deal with at this particular moment.

"April, I don't think I can make these calls. Would you do it?"

Her response was quick. "Yes."

She allowed me to go to our bedroom to watch some television and get some rest while she took care of it all. A couple of hours later, she came up to our room to let me know that everyone was contacted. There was shock and concern, but everyone seemed to take it as well as either of us could have hoped. Even my mom seemed to be okay for now. She is an impressively strong lady and would not have let April know that she was in any level of distress even if she was. I guessed that she was. I wanted to go across the street and let her see that I was okay, tell her that I was coping. I just didn't have it in me to even try. April said that my mom understood. April and I had been married nearly twenty-five years on that very memorable Monday. I knew she was a great wife, but I never dreamed I would burden her in the way that I had that day. First, I told her that her husband had cancer. Then I asked her to contact my entire family and break the news while I went to my room to watch *Judge Judy*. This was only the beginning of the many pains and sacrifices April would endure in the days and years ahead. Great wife, indeed.

I was once again in Dr. Mike's office the first thing on Tuesday morning. This time April was at my side. Dr. Tony was gracious enough to join us. His knowledge, support, and guidance would be invaluable to April and me in the coming weeks and months. The visit started as I expected. Other than my newly diagnosed condition, I was healthy. As a result, my PST was comprised of a physical exam, blood work, and measurement of the typical vital signs: blood pressure, pulse, temperature, and blood oxygen levels. All fine. Then we went into Dr. Mike's office. We reviewed my scans in detail. It didn't sound like a great story to me. As Dr. Mike had told us just the day before, the main tumor was large and had grown well outside the bounds of my kidney. There were in excess of a dozen small tumors scattered throughout my lungs. Job one was addressing the problems in my abdomen. This would be a complex procedure, and any complications removing the tumor from the vena cava could mean death. This was difficult news to hear, but Dr. Mike delivered it with compassion and the caring that—I am sure—is the reason he has so many loyal patients.

If the news of my potentially life-threatening diagnosis was the proverbial sucker punch, then what came next while April and I sat on the patient side of Dr. Mike's desk was a kick in the head. "According to the statistics, 70 percent of patients with your condition expire within three years of their diagnosis." When Dr. Mike said it, I was not sure that I heard it right. I remember my question very clearly: "You mean that even if this surgery is wildly successful, chances are that I will still die within three years?" I squeezed April's hand at exactly the same moment that she squeezed mine. I looked over at Dr. Tony who was seated a few feet away on a couch against the wall. He nodded to confirm the validity of the statement, assuring me with the calm voice of a surgeon and a friend that there were many treatments available that could affect my individual outcome. Dr. Mike concurred and went on, "Our focus right now is to get through this surgery and your recovery. We will discuss treatments later." That was the last time I thought about treatments until well after the surgery. But this was a sobering discussion.

As a hospital executive, I was well aware that a large percentage of surgical cancer patients require ongoing treatments. I approved the investment decisions we were making at Lenox Hill, investments in facilities and equipment enabling us to deliver radiation therapy and chemotherapy. I was also aware of the services we provided in the department of medical oncology where cancer patients are treated with oral and infusion medications. How could I have thought that I would not require any of those post-surgical treatments? I guess I didn't have time to consider the possibilities. I know I never thought my life could still be shortened after a successful surgery. During this short time that I was aware of my diagnosis, I guess I assumed that I would have surgery, and then things would go back to normal. Normal. My personal normal, and that of April and Madeline and Christina and so many people who knew me and cared about me would never be exactly the same again.

Wednesday morning came fast. April and I were at the hospital by 5:00 a.m. I was first up in the OR (now I knew what that meant) as Dr. Mike wanted to get a particularly early start. This procedure was going to take a while. Early was good as it also allowed me to get through the pre-op process and into the OR before very many of the other hospital employees showed up for work that day. It would be easier if I could get through the surgery seeing as few familiar faces as possible. April was at my side from the minute we awoke that morning. She literally walked me into the OR and was at my bedside when I came out of the anesthesia in the PACU; but I am getting ahead of myself.

I felt an odd sense of confidence as we entered the hospital that Wednesday morning, literally under the cover of darkness. Don't get me wrong. I was not at all pleased to be at the hospital that day, nor was I looking forward to anything that was going to happen. But I was calm and confident. We got into the elevator, and I pushed the button with the number 10 on it. I had pushed that button dozens, if not hundreds, of times in the past. This time was obviously different.

We got out on the tenth floor and proceeded through the waiting area to the registration desk. As was the case when Deb accompanied me through the same route, there were already several people sitting in the waiting area. This time I was a patient in jeans and a sweatshirt, so nobody took particular notice of me, and I did not make eye contact with any of the people seated there. Still, I noticed the same pensive looks on their faces, that same look of concern, distress, maybe even fear. My stomach did not become unsettled this time, but I did become a little sad as I thought that April would shortly be spending some number of hours waiting, likely with the same look on her face. We completed patient registration and proceeded to pre-op.

Before I knew it, I was in my hospital gown, seated in my lounge chair, awaiting my succession of visits from a variety of caregivers. Being stripped of my identity was a very real feeling, but I was expecting it and didn't allow it to bother me very much. I knew what and who was coming, and it all unfolded as I had seen it happen before. A visit from a nurse. Patient identification. A visit from the anesthesiologist. Patient identification. Another nurse. Then the same nurse who first visited me. I knew we were getting close to "game time" when Dr. Mike visited. He was in his scrubs, seemingly ready to go. He was his regular confident self, possibly a little more intense than I was used to, but I had never seen him in pre-op before. I was not concerned. We exchanged some pleasantries, and then Dr. Mike marked and autographed the surgical site, all as expected. Again, I am not attempting to suggest that this was pleasant or that I was in any way happy to be there. Still, the predictability of what was coming, my familiarity with each step in the process, and my confidence in the people that I had come to know in what was now my second home enabled me to remain calm and confident. My miracle-inspired decisions to the rescue once again!

Finally, it was time to walk the hallway from pre-op to the OR. The walk, I knew it well. The pre-op nurse accompanied me and April down the path. The loved one typically parts company with the patient in pre-op, and the patient makes this walk alone. I got a little special treatment that day, and I was pleased to be able to take the walk with April by my side. The walk was just as I remembered it. We made the lefts and the rights. We passed by the lone window, and I took one more look outside. This time it did not seem cruel at all, not like it did when I passed it during my walk with Deb. It was just one more pleasant look outside before I would arrive at the entrance to the sterile space. Pleasant! I remained calm and confident. My stomach was fine; it never became unsettled as it had that day I walked with Deb. I did not feel as if I were taking a walk to the electric chair. I didn't want to have to do it, but I knew and was confident that I was walking to the procedure that would save my life. I had hope. That hope, once again, afforded to me because of my miracle-inspired decisions.

I kissed April goodbye for now at the end of the hallway and stepped into the sterile space. Deb met me right inside the sterile area and walked me to my assigned OR. We spoke a bit, but I will admit that I was nervous enough at that point that I don't remember what we said. I climbed onto the table, watched as the last preparations and safety procedures were completed, and shortly after Dr. Mike entered the OR, the anesthesia was administered.

I barely remember my time in the PACU though I do remember that April never left my side. I likewise don't remember much about my first night and the next day in the surgical intensive care unit, other than I had tubes coming out of everywhere and almost every member of my immediate family was crammed into that room—another exception that was made for me—and my nurse was not happy about it. I really did need rest. I went home twelve days later. I was home for over four months before I returned to work, and it took me many more months to regain my strength and stamina.

I will return to my post-surgical days in later chapters. For now, I would like to explain why I described my diagnosis and surgical experience in such detail. As I hope you have come to understand, I avoided doctors and hospitals for all of my youth and most of my adult career. Had I not taken my path to healthcare and Lenox Hill, I would likely have never met Dr. Mike. I would never have progressed from symptom to surgery in five short days, and I would never have endured the challenges of Monday, Tuesday, and particularly Wednesday with confident calm. Would I still be alive today? Maybe. Would I have endured the day of surgery? For sure. Many people do who have not had the benefit of Susan's boot camp or Deb's tour day, but my diagnosis and surgery were full of too many coincidences to be the result of chance. The walk to the electric chair turning into the walk of hope, meeting Dr. Mike who taught me about the very surgical procedure he would eventually perform on me, my comfort interacting with doctors inside of hospitals. For sure, many people survive and thrive through similar experiences having none of the benefits I enjoyed from the life path I chose, but that very path prepared me for this event, and it prepared me well. During those five days and throughout my life since my surgery, I reaped the benefit of the four miracle-inspired decisions I have described to you thus far. There is more to this story. More miracle-inspired decisions and more meaningful life changes which I will share in the chapters ahead. But first, I will recap my miracle-inspired life path thus far.

CHAPTER

8

LET'S RECAP

Let's recap the four miracle-inspired decisions that I have described so far, their linkage, and how they prepared me for my diagnosis and surgery. I contend that because of the severity of my condition at diagnosis, the potential for a short-term catastrophic event, and the likelihood for delay in my receiving care had my life taken a path to any place other than Lenox Hill, that my life path actually saved my life. I respect your right to conclude otherwise. Even if you do, I find it inarguable that I benefited greatly from the life path I followed and the place where I had arrived at the time of my diagnosis.

For your consideration, following is a summary of my four miracle-inspired decisions, their linkage, and their impact on my diagnosis and surgery:

The Firm. At age twenty-one, I was well positioned to begin a career in public accounting. I had interviewed with six of the big 8 firms, and two of the firms that offered me a position were organizations that I would have happily joined. I was reluctant to visit the final firm that had invited me in for an interview, but I didn't have a credible reason for canceling. When my grandfather passed away, his funeral was scheduled for the exact same date as that interview. In order to fulfill an obligation related to the family business, I canceled that final interview with Arthur Andersen. The firm persisted, and I reluctantly rescheduled. After the interview, I received an unexpected call from the firm's partner responsible for recruiting. That exchange included an increase to his original offer in the amount of one thousand dollars, and I made a last-minute and unanticipated decision to join Arthur Andersen. I still have no rational explanation for why that decisive, hardheaded twenty-one year old made that compulsive decision. It was a miracle-inspired decision that set me on a path—a path which eventually prepared me to cope with and overcome my cancer diagnosis and surgery. You see, I was successful at Arthur Andersen. I was a good consultant, and I loved working in a partnership. Had I joined one of the other two firm, I believe that I would have been awarded partnership and that I would have likely stayed in that business. There was one big difference with Arthur Andersen. It was the only one of the Big 8 firms that was to meet an unlikely demise. It was the only one of the firms that would force me to leave and pursue a career elsewhere. My miracle-inspired decision to join Arthur Andersen is directly linked to my need to make a career change. But there were several directions I could have taken. How would I decide?

Healthcare. I was enjoying a successful consulting career assisting health insurance companies to integrate their operations after executing their merger and acquisition transactions. When it became time to reinvent my consulting career, I was asked to build a healthcare practice in the northeast region. After reviewing with Eric a long list of cons and a very short list of pros, I made the miracle-inspired decision to start that healthcare practice. I made that decision against my better judgment; it made me personally uncomfortable to work with doctors and to be inside hospitals, and I knew that Lou did not support the creation of a healthcare practice within our consulting business. Shortly after, Arthur Andersen was forced to close its doors; but there had been enough time for me to establish my credentials and relationships in healthcare. So while it was joining Arthur Andersen that ultimately drove me to change careers, it was my decision to consult to the healthcare industry that created the opportunity for me to consider a role with a health system.

Northwell. After leaving Arthur Andersen, I attempted to continue my consulting career at BearingPoint. There was much work to be done to integrate the BC professionals into our new environment. When it came time to determine my long-term role, I was awarded a leadership role in the health insurance practice. Within the first year, I concluded that BearingPoint was not the right place for me. I had time to look. I was not yet receiving any pressure for my lackluster performance. I had options; there were other consulting firms, and I was still a licensed certified public accountant. When an opportunity presented itself at Northwell, I decided to pursue it. I attended a couple of "interviews" and was offered a position to run the revenue cycle operation. Similar to the situation I was presented when Eric asked me to start the healthcare practice in BC, the list of cons was long, and the list of pros was short. After my brief yet thorough analysis, I concluded that I would not join Northwell; I would continue to look. April agreed. When Bob called me back with an adjusted offer which still represented a significant pay decrease, I made the miracle-inspired decision to accept a role at Northwell. This decision brought me one big step closer to Lenox Hill. Remember: I was only *able* to make this miracle-inspired decision because I said yes to starting a healthcare practice. I only *had* to make this miracle-inspired decision because I joined Arthur Andersen.

Lenox Hill. I could never work in a hospital. They scared me, and doctors made me nervous. In my early years with Northwell, I was able to avoid doctors and spent as little time as possible actually inside the hospitals. When I started at Northwell, I was running the hospital revenue cycle. Soon after, the medical group revenue cycle was added to my responsibilities, and I was compelled to become more comfortable working and interacting with doctors. Within a few years, I was appointed CFO of our two largest tertiary hospitals. I met Susan who persisted until I became comfortable rounding the hospital units, interacting with doctors, nurses, and eventually, patients. I asked for an assignment where I could once again run an operation. My rounding with Susan became a boot camp, and within a few months, I was asked to go into Manhattan to run Lenox Hill. This time, my miracle-inspired decision to say yes was not the result of a last-minute or unexpected event; it was the culmination of several years of career progression. That progression seemed unremarkable as it occurred, but it systematically eliminated the barriers that existed within myself to ever being able to work full-time inside a hospital. I ran the medical group revenue cycle which forced me to learn to interact with doctors; I met a boss that pushed me out of my comfort zone into the halls of the hospital; and I interacted with a patient who surely impacted me more than I did him. This miracle-inspired decision was the most complicated manipulation of time and events that God weaved into my life. It was the final step in my then twenty-six-year career that brought me to the place where I would become psychologically prepared for my diagnosis and surgery, where I would meet Dr. Mike months before my diagnosis, and where I would learn about my surgical procedure from the doctor who would eventually perform it.

So there you have it. Four miracle-inspired decisions, each of which on their own is arguably an unremarkable step in the progression of a typical professional career. However, when linked together, these decisions created a life path that prepared me in an incredible way for the biggest challenge of my life. When I consider the circumstances that surrounded these decisions—my personal tendencies, my normal decision-making process, even my worries and fears—they become anything but unremarkable. I am convinced that only through God's inspiration, through His manipulation of the time and events, could I possibly have made the decisions that I made.

I have so far shared with you four of the six miracle-inspired decisions. The remaining two miracle-inspired decisions are different from the first four in two ways: first, they have nothing to do with my job and my career, they are decisions that I and April made in our personal lives; and second, they most affected my life after my diagnosis and surgery as opposed to preparing me for my diagnosis and surgery. I will share these last two miracle-inspired decisions in the chapters that follow.

A Home in the Mountains

Through the first eight chapters of this book, I have shared with you my miracle-inspired path through my work life—an unlikely career track—at least for me, from accountant to hospital executive director where I met the doctor that saved my life. I have come to realize that my career path was not the only path I was traveling. My life has been more complicated than that; I was traveling multiple paths simultaneously. Each path had its own miracle-inspired decisions. Each of those decisions set me in a direction that led me to another life decision that, with God's inspiration, guided me to a place where I never would have anticipated I would have landed. In each case, that place I landed opened up possibilities for me to deal with my life challenges in a way I would never have been able to had I not come to that particular place in my life.

My intention in the pages that follow is to share with you two more miracle-inspired decisions. These decisions levied a profound impact on my personal life. Like the four I have already shared with you, these were unlikely decisions inspired by the timing of unexpected events which prepared me to cope and thrive with my life challenges. For sure, these decisions do not define my entire personal life path; in reality, they occurred and have impacted only about five or so of my fifty-five years. I suspect that if you consider your own life, you will find that you too have traveled multiple and simultaneous paths. As we are moving from my career to my personal path, I will need to insert you into the time and place when these last two decisions occurred, so you can best appreciate these events and the intersection of my personal life path with the four miracle-inspired decisions I made in my career life.

It was 2008. My career was back on track. Working at Northwell since 2004, I had logged successes in my revenue cycle work for both the hospital and the medical group. I was appointed CFO of the tertiary facilities, and my very important relationship with Susan was beginning to develop. I had not yet received my diagnosis. Life at home was also progressing as any happy family could hope. Sure, we had our challenges like every other family, but April and I were and continue to be in a loving and supportive relationship. Christina was nearing the end of her college career, a marketing major at Pace University in Manhattan. She was and still is an incredibly driven person, and her career plans were shaping nicely. She was interning at a marketing firm and planned a full-time job there at graduation. She eventually landed that position and has been blessed to have an exciting and fulfilling career in her young life. She has since made a couple of career changes and is currently a successful real estate agent in the competitive Manhattan market. Currently twenty-seven, I suspect that she will look back in a number of years and realize that she has already made some miracle-inspired decisions in her young life.

Madeline was finishing up her sophomore year at Fordham University in the Bronx. She was an accounting major and an excellent student. She had adjusted to college and campus life smoothly. She had aspirations of joining one of, what was now, the Big 4 firms. I had little doubt that she would achieve that goal in a similar fashion that her dad had some twenty-five-plus years earlier. In fact, she did a few years later. After a graduate year at Fordham's Manhattan campus, she joined PriceWaterhouseCoopers (PWC), one of the Big 4, and became a certified public accountant. She had become a free spirit—an unlikely combination of, at times, loner and at other times incredibly giving and involved person. I am proud of both of my daughters now as I was back in 2008 when April and I could see their energy for life and the respective futures that dwelled inside them both.

Work and home life were great, so April and I had, for the first time in our lives, both the time and the budget to start thinking about a second home for weekend solace and vacation getaways. For my entire young life, my parents owned a second home in Upstate New York, a village called Saugerties. The village was quaint though somewhat economically depressed for virtually the entire time my parents owned their home. That didn't matter much because the real attraction to the area was the rural surrounding that was the town of Saugerties. My parents' home sat on twenty-five acres in the wooded valley of the Catskill mountains. There, my dad hunted deer and rabbits during the colder weather with his brothers and his friends, and family time was spent mostly in the warmer weather, tending the grounds, barbecuing, and enjoying the country. There were day trips to the local attractions. It was a welcome change for a family from Brooklyn.

In 2008, April and I enjoyed skiing and were considering golf lessons. When considering the place for our second home, the mountains was a logical decision, but not Saugerties. We were looking for a place that was a little more upscale, not so economically depressed, with a variety of restaurants, and some night life. A local friend of ours, Matt, told us about a place in the Pocono mountains of Pennsylvania. It was a private development called Evergreen Ridge. Building lots were available for sale, so we could construct a custom home. There was a championship eighteen-hole golf course, a nine-hole executive golf course under construction, horseback riding, skiing, pools, stocked lakes, community space, dining, and activities for any age group—all within the gated and private community. It was very much what we were looking for. We drove the three-hour trip from our home in Brooklyn to Evergreen Ridge. The drive was pleasant, and the community was very nice. The buildings and amenities were brand-new. The development was still being expanded, and all indications were that properties were selling well. There were plenty of homes already built. We took a golf lesson and sampled the restaurant. We very much enjoyed the experience. We met with a salesperson; it was the typical hard sell you would expect in a development or time-share community. We didn't mind much, and despite the pressures inherent in Evergreen Ridge's sales process, we took the time we needed and eventually made the decision to purchase an empty lot overlooking the nine-hole golf course which would open in the spring of 2009. We visited Evergreen Ridge frequently, taking golf lessons into the fall and enjoying the ski area into the winter of 2009. We enjoyed all of these activities available right within the community, and April and I were pleased to find out that the lot to the left of the one we already purchased was available. We purchased that lot and now owned a half acre on the golf course. Spring was soon to arrive, and we set our sights on the home we would build. Things were beginning to move quickly, and that was fine by me. This felt right.

The decision to build was big for April and me. I was excited, but this would be the biggest single investment we will ever have made, including the purchase of our primary residence some fifteen years earlier. We did our diligence. We researched the contractors that were approved to build at Evergreen Ridge. We talked to several of them and obtained books full of blueprints and pictures of the various homes for us to consider. We poured through those plans, considering the layouts, number of bedrooms and bathrooms, and the price per square foot each would cost across the various contractors. After much consideration, we selected the home we wanted. It was four bedrooms and three bathrooms. The sizable kitchen was completely open to the dining and living rooms, which included a wood-burning fireplace. April and I thought through dozens of details, keeping a list of the things we hoped might be included in the plan and another list of things we assumed would be extras. We flipped through the book of blueprints time and time again even after we had selected the home that we wanted, just to make sure that there wasn't another one that we might like better. We were fairly certain that we had worked out exactly what we wanted. A fine traditional home, right around twenty-five hundred square feet, with a finished basement. We estimated what this would all cost and made sure our notes were all together. We were ready. Joe was the contractor we wanted to work with, and we scheduled a Saturday afternoon to meet him at the Evergreen Ridge hotel to begin planning.

April and I were eager to meet with Joe. We brought our plans, our notes, and our checkbook as we anticipated hiring Joe that day. We had screened enough contractors, Joe came highly recommended, and he was coming prepared to show us some of the other properties he had already completed within Evergreen Ridge and to provide references.

It was a beautiful early spring day when we met with Joe. Trees were coming back to life, and the spring flowers were beginning to bud. Still, there was a slight chill in the air while the sun shone brightly. Perfect spring day in my book. We waited for Joe to arrive in the large common space right behind the hotel lobby. The room was grand. Bulky wood-framed chairs with soft cushions were scattered around the space, except where they were neatly arranged to optimize the area around the oversized stone fireplace which stretched the entire length to the second story ceiling. Diagonally across from the fireplace was a balcony and walkway where hotel guests headed to their second-floor rooms looked down as they walked by. There were several pub-style tables scattered around the room, each with four bar stools carefully spaced around them. April and I had chosen one of those tables and got seated for our meeting with Joe. The entire room was decorated and adorned to remind you that you were in the mountains: rustic wooden accents, antique brass lamps, and oversized chandeliers. There were sconces made from deer antlers deliberately spaced around the entire room. The focal point of the entire space was the back wall which was floor to ceiling windows and glass doors. The hotel was built on the slope of the mountain, so the deck outside the glass doors was at least a couple of stories above the ground below even though the entrance to the hotel was at ground level in front. The view from any one of those bulky chairs was breathtaking: rolling hills with a mountain backdrop. Trees and multicolored wild shrubs dotted the landscape. Every imaginable shade of green adorned the rolling hills. The blue sky finished the painting-quality view with its white puffy clouds and brilliant sun tucked between the mountaintops. An occasional hawk floated across the landscape in search of its next meal, one of the few reminders that this was a live scene and not some oil on canvas. I definitely liked it here. This felt right.

Joe arrived on time. He was professional and friendly. He looked like a contractor: neat jeans, flannel shirt, a small portfolio in his hand. He looked old enough to me to be trusted yet young enough that I could relate to him. Initial impression: approved. After a few minutes of pleasantries, we got down to business. April and I unfolded our portfolio of materials. The books, the notes, the blueprint we had selected—Joe could not see even a single square inch of the surface of the pub table. We engaged in detailed and productive discussion for an hour or more. We showed Joe the house we had selected. We went through our lists, keeping track of what would be an extra and what was already included in the plan. Several of the items required a degree of discussion, but virtually all that we wanted seemed possible, and none looked to be too much of a budget challenge. I was beginning to like Joe. I could feel the checkbook tucked into my back pocket and was anticipating the moment that I would shake Joe's hand and write him a check to secure his services.

Our discussion paused for a moment. The generally friendly look on Joe's face became slightly more serious. It became immediately clear, as Joe leaned back in his seat, that he had a few questions for us. I didn't know it then, but April and I were about to get set up for a miracle-inspired decision.

For the next fifteen minutes or so, Joe, April, and I engaged in a discussion that was driven by a set of intriguing, even controversial, questions delivered in a matter-of-fact manner by Joe. To be clear, there were times that Joe was informing, times he was encouraging, and times he was clearly sending a warning signal. For a time, he came across as a father figure. I got the sense that he was speaking as a man who had a portfolio of dissatisfied customers through no fault of his own, dissatisfied not because he built them a bad house, dissatisfied for some other reason or set of reasons that were somehow out of his control. His questions through which he drove the next fifteen minutes of discussion went something like this:

"The house you selected is a little too small. You have a property on the golf course, and the development has a minimum square footage for homes on the golf course. We will need to add just over one hundred square feet. It would be easy on this plan to just make the living and dining area larger. Would you be okay with that?"

"You mentioned that you are interested in a clear view of the golf course. We can clear the property for you, but the development must approve the removal of any trees in excess of six inches in diameter. They are usually accommodating in situations like yours, but I cannot guarantee that we will be able to remove all the trees that you want us to. Okay?"

"The development requires that all homes in your area be faced with stone on the front. You have some options to choose from, but it has to be stone. You can use siding on the back and sides if you choose. Okay?"

"You mentioned that you like to tend to your own lawn and garden. The development does not allow sheds or other outbuildings in your area, so any equipment will need to be stored in your garage. Okay?"

There were a couple of more rules and restrictions. To be honest, I shut down after this first round of what I considered to be bombs!

When Joe was done with his list of questions, it was time for April and me to lean back in our seats, which we did in tandem, with absolutely no signaling to each other. I imagine that we both had the same bewildered look on our faces. I could tell from the look on Joe's face, it said to me: "mission accomplished." Without very much more discussion, we thanked Joe for his time, he packed up his neat folio, and after we told him that we would be in touch, he left. My checkbook remained securely in my back pocket. I remember being so shaken by the experience that I took my thumb and pressed the checkbook as deeply into my back pocket as it would go, as if that extra tuck would provide assurance that I would not take it out and spontaneously write a big check to Joe as he walked away through the hotel lobby.

April and I looked at each other in disbelief. We had just had the wind taken out of our sails, and without saying a word to each other, we each knew what the other was thinking, and it was exactly what we were each thinking ourselves: Who is this "development," and why does he, she, or they think that they get to tell us how big our house will be or what our house will look like or where we will store our lawn mower? Granted, the development was beautiful, and I guess you need standards to keep it that way, but we paid a premium for those lots with a view of the golf course. Wouldn't it have been the right thing for our salesman to let us know that our view might be limited by some of the larger trees on the lots? Trees that the "development" would decide whether they would stay or go? I lived in private homes my entire life, and April and I have owned our homes since we were married. Neither of us were sure that we were going to be happy here.

We sat for a while longer. We spoke, but not very much. Once we had confirmed for each other that we were thinking exactly the same thing, there was not a lot more to say. I stared out the wall of windows at the back of the room. The buds were still budding, and the sun was still shining, but the view was not quite as captivating as it was just a couple of hours earlier. It was not very captivating at all anymore. The room in which we were seated was still grand and beautifully decorated, but it no longer had a warm country feeling. This no longer felt right. Within the span of fifteen minutes, both April and I went from being excited to talk to the contractor that we were about ready to hire to build our custom country getaway to dejected and disappointed to have come to the realization that Evergreen Ridge was not for us. The emotional swing from very high to very low was exhausting.

What about Joe? Who was this guy? I considered myself to be a fairly accomplished businessman, but I was genuinely excited as we talked about this house. Joe had to see that I was ready to make a deal. Why would a contractor drop a small pile of hand grenades when what he should have been doing was closing his deal? I could have been right that he was tired of building great homes for dissatisfied customers, his parting words to us, after he saw the astonishment in our faces, did include advice that we think about the pros and cons of development living. Still, this was not normal behavior, and I remain confident that there was some level of divine intervention in our selection of Joe as our potential contractor.

Intervention, perhaps, but selecting Joe was not the miracle-inspired decision that I am intending to describe to you. You see, before April and I left our seats, we decided that we would not build at Evergreen Ridge and that we would look elsewhere for our weekend getaway. We would hold the property for a while and sell it when the timing was right. As I write these words some eight years later, we still own those two empty lots on the golf course at Evergreen Ridge. It turns out that they are harder to sell than they are to build on. I think that it was a good decision for April and me to look elsewhere, but more importantly, I am confident that the decision was miracle inspired. As occurred in several of the prior miracle-inspired decisions I have described, God once again manipulated specific events and their timing which caused me and April to make a last-minute decision that was very different than we originally planned. We never looked back. We never wondered if we had made the right decision.

After a brief call to Joe where I thanked him for his candor and informed him that we would not be going forward with our project, we never gave it a second thought. I am fairly certain that our meeting with Joe was the last time we ever visited Evergreen Ridge. We have heard from Matt and the occasional call from a sales representative that the place is looking great and that homes continue to get built. April and I are happy for those new homeowners and hope that they consulted with someone like Joe before they broke ground. As for us, April and I would still look for a home in the country. That search introduced us to new friends and a component of our support structure that would be invaluable once I received my diagnosis.

CHAPTER

10

"What Have You Got to Lose?"

After our experience at Evergreen Ridge, April and I were disappointed but still determined to find the right place for our weekend getaway and vacation home. As another winter approached, we had a more timely challenge to deal with first: Where would we ski for the winter of 2010/2011? I had skied at various resorts in Pennsylvania, Vermont, and New York. The goal was to find a place we would enjoy that was close enough to our home in Brooklyn that we would be interested in making the trip as many weekends between December and March that we were free from other commitments. If prior ski seasons were to be a good gauge, that would be as many as three weekends per month. The closest resort that had a good variety of trails and amenities was Hunter Mountain in Upstate New York. I had skied at Hunter in the past; my parents' vacation home/hunting getaway in Saugerties was about forty-five minutes south of the resort. We decided to give Hunter a chance for the upcoming season. Madeline also enjoyed skiing from time to time, and she joined us on several of the weekends that season. Somewhat to our surprise, we very much enjoyed our experience at Hunter. They had expanded the number of trails and the amenities in the thirty-plus years since I had skied there last. They opened a family center where signing up for lessons and obtaining rental equipment were easy and quick.

While there were still a lot of "hard core" skiers and "hot doggers" on day trips from New York City, the crowd was more mixed than I remembered, and the increased percentage of families and children gave the mountain more of a friendly feel.

As ski season approached and throughout that winter, April and I made the most of our trips north. We visited the villages that surround the resort and learned the shops and restaurants in the area. We also visited the three main villages south of Hunter: Kingston, Woodstock, and Saugerties. Once you have come down the mountain into the valley, these three villages are within ten or twelve miles of each other. Each has its own unique personality. Kingston is by far the largest of the three. More a city than a village, Kingston was once the state capital of New York. It is full of history and its share of stately buildings to prove it. I presume it is because of this history that it is the most densely populated, has the most shopping, and among the widest variety of restaurants from which to choose. Woodstock is Woodstock. It is the famous sight, in name at least, of the weekend long music festival in 1969 that attracted over four hundred thousand people. It inspired the name of the mischievous yellow bird who befriended Snoopy in the *Peanuts* cartoons. It is the artsy little town where the main strip is packed solid with tourists from Memorial Day to Labor Day enjoying the shops, the art, and the eclectic group of locals you can only find in Woodstock. Completing the triangle is Saugerties. The little village approximately ten miles north of Kingston, approximately the same distance east of Woodstock, and just minutes from the Hudson River. Without much industry or a historic reputation to attract tourists, Saugerties, though quaint, was depressed for the three or so decades my parents owned their home.

Main Street crosses Partition Street at the heart of the village. As a teenager, I remember looking down both streets from their intersection and thinking that this village must have had a "hay day" at some point in its history when these neatly appointed buildings with their second-story facades were beautiful. I imagined what the village looked like when the detailed work in these building facades was new, fresh, and painted in multicolors, when the open porch of the small hotel on the corner was well maintained, and guests sat on rocking chairs, drinking their lemonade on a hot sunny afternoon. I imagined that this village could have been a pretty little town from the old west with horse-drawn carriages, men in ties and top hats, and women in hoop skirts. I also remember thinking that those days were long gone and that this little village had seen its best days. The facades were faded and crumbling; most of the businesses were lower-end garment stores or "antique" shops. There was virtually no family entertainment or dining except for the small and outdated movie theater at the end of Main Street. Even in the summer, the sidewalks were relatively empty, particularly when compared to the crowded streets of Woodstock.

The decades that passed since my last visit to Main Street brought amazing change and improvement to the village. Saugerties had become a horse town. A local resident of the village converted over two hundred acres of property on the edge of the village into one of our nation's largest horse show and jumping facilities. The complex has the capacity to house a couple of thousand horses that, together with their owners, their riders, and spectators, visit Saugerties in large waves from Wednesday through Sunday every week from Memorial Day through Labor Day. The events attract thousands of visitors, particularly when the prize money reaches its peak of one million dollars. The impact on the village has been remarkable. Tourists flood the streets of the village during the peak season. Restaurants, pubs, and night life abound in the village and the surrounding area, servicing thousands of visitors each and every week during the summer. Tired storefronts have been refurbished, filled with boutiques, specialty shops, and fine dining. A luxury hotel and catering facility was constructed where an abandoned factory used to sit. The view from the corner of Main and Partition is fresh, alive, and refurbished. There aren't any horse-drawn carriages, but the village now sees its share of high-end luxury automobiles.

I was amazed at the transformation. It took several months of weekends to sample the fare at the most popular restaurants that dot the streets of the village and rural roads of the surrounding town. Multiple golf courses had been built within ten miles of Saugerties, at least one of them is a championship eighteen-hole course. April and I very much enjoyed our visits to the Saugerties area where we realized that all of the hobbies and passtimes we enjoyed were available to us. We could ski, golf, and hunt, as well as find fine dining, theater, and concerts, all within a short ride from what had become a very happening village. Though we had written off this little village only a couple of years earlier, we decided that Saugerties would become our weekend getaway and vacation destination.

When we began our search, we were not sure exactly which area we liked best to target for our new home. There were many benefits to locating right within the village, which has a beautiful residential area within walking distance of Main and Partition. Outside the village is the town of Saugerties which is much more rural with winding roads, wooded space, and plenty of wildlife. West Saugerties is a portion of the town which is midway between the villages of Saugerties and Woodstock, placing you less than ten miles from both. There were areas east of the village where homes provide breathtaking views of the Hudson River. The possibilities abound. Our approach was simple. We drove around the residential streets of the village and the winding roads of the town looking for "For Sale" signs and writing down the broker phone numbers for the places that looked interesting. We then debated the different areas and decided that the first place we would look at was a neat wood-framed home within the village, with a front porch and that, from the outside, looked to be recently renovated. The agent with which we would work would be the one that picked up the phone when we called the number from the "For Sale" sign on the front of that house. An agent answered my call promptly. He sounded professional and friendly. I inquired about the house and made an appointment for the following Saturday. The agent's name was George, and we were to meet him in front of the neat wood-framed house with the porch early that Saturday morning.

April was a real estate agent when I met her. Christina is currently a real estate agent. I love them both and believe them both to be moral people with a high degree of integrity. That is where my love for real estate agents ends. I have met a number of agents over the years; I have been involved in nearly a dozen purchase and sale transactions, most of them related to private residences. I have had productive relationships with real estate agents. I have even met a number of them that I have liked and enjoyed doing business with, but I never met any that I really trusted, that I believed was genuinely more committed to my interests as a client than their interest in making the sale. That was true, at least until I met George.

I would best describe George as a gentle giant. I am six feet tall, and George is meaningfully taller than I am. I have never asked him, but I would guess that he is at least six feet four or six feet five inches tall. A number of years older than me, he has a full head of flowing gray hair, broad shoulders, and big hands. His rugged look allows him to fit into the rural surroundings of Saugerties quite well. He often wears his signature leather vest along with a collared shirt, neat jeans, and leather boots. His innate personality traits earned my respect as they are so unusual when compared with those of other real estate agents I have met: calm, patient, genuinely and consistently friendly, transparent, and collaborative. I trusted him when he told me that an offer I was willing to make was too low because he shared his rationale and also because he told me when an offer I was willing to make was too high. For any given property, he would tell me the ask price, the price at which he thought it would sell, and at what price we should start. If I wanted to offer less or cap out at a price lower than he recommended, he never argued with me or pressured me. He advised, and he was right more times than he was wrong.

There were plenty of properties on which to test his skills and observe his approach. April and I must have looked at two or three dozen properties with George over the several months that followed that Saturday morning when we met him at that little wood-framed home in the village. We looked at other homes in the village and homes in the town, homes with acreage around them, and homes on relatively small parcels. We saw properties with grand views of the Hudson River, homes with docks on the Esopus Creek, and even a parcel that included a small house, a barn, horse paddock, and pond. April and I didn't know exactly what we wanted, and we planned on seeing everything we could before we made a decision. George worked with us weekend after weekend; he never lost interest in us, and he never got tired of debating value and price. We made some low-ball offers on properties we were mildly interested in, and we negotiated hard for a massive log cabin we liked but thought was overpriced. We didn't get that log cabin, but it sat on the market for months because it was in fact overpriced.

April and I had gotten a rather strong sense of the market when George called us about a twenty-four hundred square foot cape cod style home on about two acres on a private road. We were skiing at Hunter that weekend and made the trip down to the valley on a sunny but cold Sunday morning after a nor'easter had dropped over a foot of fresh snow across the area. My initial impression was luke-warm. I was not excited about a cape cod, and both April and I were thinking about purchasing a home with a little more property, but George had a good sense of what we liked, and he assured me that this one would be worth the trip down the mountain in the fresh snow. So we drove the ten or so miles that took us nearly an hour on the slick roads.

Both April and I were pleasantly surprised. The house was in great condition. It had a large kitchen that was just open enough to the dining room. Two bathrooms and four bedrooms were sufficient for our needs, and it was a big plus that one of those bedrooms was on the first floor, so my mom would be comfortable when she vis-ited, and it could also be used as an office or den. The house had a finished basement, central air-conditioning, a backup generator, a large outside deck, a three-season room, and a gentle brook babbling along the rear property line. It had just about all we were looking for. April sat on the steps that were nicely placed just inside the front door, and we discussed our offer strategy with George. Before we left the property, we had settled on our opening offer, and we parted company with George knowing exactly how we wanted him to nego-tiate the deal and the highest price we would be willing to pay.

We closed the deal that very next Tuesday at a price that was within our predetermined range. By early spring we had closed on the property, and by summer our weekend getaway was freshly painted and fully furnished. That was 2011, and we began spending as many weekends as we possibly could in Saugerties. We started tak-

NOW I KNOW I AM NOT ALONE

ing golf lessons, and we purchased new ski equipment. I was working at Lenox Hill at the time; April would meet me there on the Upper East Side of Manhattan on Friday afternoons, and we would take the George Washington Bridge and head north for the two-hour drive to Saugerties. We became quickly attached to our vacation home and wanted to make sure we could tend to any issues that might arise as timely as possible. George agreed to hold a key in the event we needed someone to get to the house during the week while April and I were in Brooklyn. To date, we have only had to bother him once for what turned out to be a false alarm. George had become a good and trusted friend as well as our real estate agent. To this day he holds our key, and we routinely enjoy dinner with him and Jan, George's "better half."

Life was good. My career was going well, and I enjoyed my work at Lenox Hill. Christina and Madeline were doing well in college. April and I were enjoying the outdoors and were more physically fit than we had been in decades. It was just over a year after we purchased the home in Saugerties when I received my cancer diagnosis in July of 2012. April and I spent blocks of a week at a time in Saugerties during my slow but steady recovery that fall. It was during one of those trips that I had the occasion to talk to George. He was clearly shaken by the news of my diagnosis and asked that we get together. He had something that he wanted to talk to me about, but it had to be in person. Whatever it was, this was not a conversation that I could convince George to even begin over the phone. George's urging certainly peeked my curiosity, but important conversation or not, April and I were always up for a dinner with George and Jan, so we picked a night and made a dinner reservation. I didn't know it at the time—there was no way I could have—but I was getting prepped for my sixth and final miracle-inspired decision that was to happen a few short months after our dinner.

Our dinner engagement started out a little awkward. This never happened before as the four of us were very comfortable together, and we never found ourselves at a loss for easy conversation. This time was different. George started talking about his years as a youth and how things happen that you can't anticipate. He also described how things always seemed to work out, and I remember hints of divine intervention in his accounting of his early years; but they were more indirect references than any bold statement or conviction. I was becoming increasingly curious as to why George had requested a face-to-face meeting so that he could subject himself to what started out as an uncomfortable conversation and quickly became an even more uncomfortable monologue. At first, I thought he was attempting to deliver a misguided pep talk intended to help me through my difficult diagnosis. After fifteen minutes or so, his intentions became clear.

George was attempting to persuade me to meet an acquaintance of his: a healer. I didn't know what a healer was or what they did. George told me about several people who had visited this healer with rather amazing results. These people were friends and others close to George, people that he assured me were telling the truth and were not exaggerating. People close enough to him that he actually saw the results. One such case involved a person who was diagnosed with cataracts. The condition became progressively worse, and the person was afraid to have the necessary surgery. It was not long before the person was unable to drive, and driving was necessary to this person's livelihood. After several visits to this healer, the person's cataracts were gone. He was healed, no surgery necessary. They were gone, and they never returned. Another case George told me about was a friend of his who had a sudden and rather serious heart attack. He was rushed to the hospital and treated medically. The healer rode in the ambulance with the man and worked on him throughout the entire ride. To his doctor's surprise, the patient has no damage to his heart and no lasting effects from his heart attack. Yet another case was a person who had an undiagnosed condition that caused his hands to shake. The situation worsened to the point where it was very noticeable to others, and it was affecting his routine daily activities. After several visits to the healer, the man's hands stopped shaking. George explained how he himself witnessed this phenomenon.

When George was finished telling me his stories, he handed me the healer's phone number. He could tell I had been uneasy about the discussion over the prior forty-five minutes or so, yet he encouraged me, "make the call." "I will think about it" was the best I could prom-ise. I was happy and relieved when the subject of our dinner discus-sion changed and we were able to bounce from topic to topic in the relaxed fashion I was much more accustomed to from our prior visits with George and Jan. After dinner, we walked together to our cars, and George did not make any further reference to the healer. That made me happy, and he too seemed content not returning to that topic that seemed to make each of us in our own way uncomfortable.

On our ride back to the house, April and I discussed the con-versation about the healer. It turned out that the discussion was far more uncomfortable for me than it was for April. Remember, I stud-ied accounting in college and received my early training as an audi-tor; and I was a good one. I didn't believe anything that I could not see. Logic always prevailed in my thinking and, while I practiced my Catholic faith throughout my life, I believed miracles happened only in the Bible or when the pope and cardinals studied them and deemed them to be credible. In my mind, miracles didn't happen every day, and they certainly didn't happen through a "healer." Even if they did, I never experienced anything that was remotely divine or supernatural in my life, and I did not believe that a miracle would ever happen to me. Yes, even though I had already traveled my path from Arthur Andersen to healthcare, to Lenox Hill, Dr. Mike and the ORs, I had not yet connected any of these events together nor had I recognized the inspirations that drove my decisions along this path. That happened a few years later, and I will explain how that occurred in later chapters.

I was the one that started the conversation with April on the ride back from the restaurant. That conversation started something like this: "So, can you believe all those stories that George told us? I never took George to be someone who would believe in a healer." We hadn't spoken for more than a minute or two before it became clear to me that April and I were viewing this from very different perspec-tives. I thought it was crazy; I think I even referred to is as voodoo medicine. I did not believe any mere mortal could heal another with-out surgery or medicine. "What kind of person would scam people when they are at their most vulnerable?" It made me angry. April, on the other hand, was more open to the possibilities. "George is a trusted friend, and he seemed very sincere. We both believe that miracles happen, so who's to say how they happen, when they happen, where they happen?" Our thirty-minute drive was not enough time for either of us to persuade the other to their point of view. During the entire ride, I could somehow feel the piece of crumpled paper in my back pocket that had the phone number scribbled on it. I didn't want it there. I threw it away as soon as we got back to the house. As we pulled into the garage, both April and I got quiet; and when we got into the house, we put on the television, and none of our discussions throughout the rest of that week brought us back to the topic of the healer.

The several months that followed went by quickly. In early October, I was admitted to the hospital to undergo a treatment for the tumors that persisted in my lungs. I spent two weeks in the intensive care unit receiving infusion medication approximately every eight hours around the clock. Late October brought Superstorm Sandy to the New York area, and both my and my mom's house incurred meaningful damage. The cleanup and repair took weeks. In December, I went back to work after four months of disability. The year-end holidays came and went, and as I slowly regained my stamina, April and I enjoyed a long and snowy ski season. It was late winter and time to go for a CT scan to determine if the infusion treatments I had received in October were effective.

I was optimistic. This treatment had proven effective for a very small percentage of patients that chose it, but it was the only treatment that could possibly eliminate the remaining cancer in my body. It was the only treatment that was considered to be a possible cure. I had been praying for months that I would be one of those patients in that small percentage that would experience this treatment's success. I had scores of family and friends and scores of their family and friends praying for me as well. If the tumors in my lungs were not completely gone, I was anticipating that they would be smaller and far fewer in number. The news, however, was not good. Not only were the tumors still in my lungs, but the ones that were detected when I was diagnosed had grown. Some were nearly twice the size that they were originally. There were also new tumors that were not detected on the scan that was done on the day I was diagnosed. The treatment was not effective, and the disease had progressed. The progression was described in clinical terms as "remarkable."

When I got home, I met April in the kitchen in the very same spot that I had told her the news of my diagnosis some seven months earlier. I didn't know it then, but I was about to make my sixth and—for purposes of this book—final miracle-inspired decision. I was experiencing the gamut of emotions. I was angry that God had not answered my prayers. I was scared that the tumors that were growing inside my body would soon kill me like they do for the majority of people that are afflicted with this terrible and unpredictable disease. I was sad to think that my life might get cut short at this juncture where everything else—every single other thing—was going so well. I was equally sad that my death would cause such grief to April and Christina and Madeline and my brothers and my sister and to all my family and friends who were praying for me and to my mom—no mother should ever have to bury her child. I know some mothers who have, and it causes a horrible pain that never seems to go away. I began to cry again like I did in that very spot some seven months earlier. At one point I slapped the table in anger. I was angry because that treatment I had endured, the treatment that kept me in the intensive care unit for two weeks, the treatment that was my only hope for a cure, the treatment that was so toxic that it in-and-of-itself could have killed me, had not worked.

My next step was to find a new oncologist that specialized in some of the more conventional treatments and start again. I had to start all over again with oral treatments. These treatments would be in the form of a pill taken once or twice per day. These new treatments held some hope, but it was a different kind of hope. The objective of these treatments would be to stop the growth of the tumors for a period of time—on average, nine or so months—or at least slow their growth. When one treatment stops working, you try another one, and then another one. These treatments were found to be effective for a greater percentage of patients that take them than the treatment that had just failed me, but cure was not an observed outcome of these treatments, and nine months is not a long time. This was a lot to digest—a lot to accept. I felt even more vulnerable now than when I was diagnosed. I felt more mortal; I felt weaker; and I thought it was now far more likely that I would be one of those 70 percent of patients that would succumb to this disease by its third anniversary, which was now only about two years away.

April and I talked about all that was going through my mind and also what was going through hers. It was a rough moment for both of us, and neither of us was particularly encouraged by the next steps we would travel together on this journey. After a while, we both got quiet. April spoke again first. "Why don't you call the healer?" The healer? I had not thought about the healer for several months. My first reaction was not a good one. The thought of turning to a healer and expecting a miracle sparked anger within me. I had gone directly to God praying for months for my miracle. If He hadn't already cured me, why would I get my cure by going to a healer? A healer. Voodoo medicine. Ridiculous. I lashed out angrily, "It would just be a waste of money." We both got quiet again.

April again spoke first. "Frank, what do you have to lose? Just go once. It can't hurt. What do you have to lose?" I wanted to get angry again, but I did not; I am not sure why. How could I argue with her logic? I was about to go find another doctor who would prescribe some pretty rough medication with a long list of side effects that would plague me for the rest of my life. What harm would it do for me to make one visit to this healer?

"Okay, I'll go." Just minutes earlier, I had reaffirmed in my mind and to April that I believed in this healer no more now than I did when George first told me about him. I still thought it was ridiculous and a waste of time and money. But I was not angry anymore. Within a few moments, I made a one-hundred-and-eighty-degree turn from an angry "no" to a calm "yes."

As is the case in all of my miracle-inspired decisions, I cannot tell you why I said yes, and I cannot tell you in this particular case why I was no longer angry. Surprising to me at the time, I felt it was the right thing for me to do the moment I said yes. I had long since thrown away George's piece of paper that contained the name and phone number for the healer. I called George and asked him for the number again. I scratched it onto yet another scrap of paper. I explained to George that I had decided to visit his healer. He was very pleased. Some six months after he had told April and me his incredible stories, George was pleased. As I hung up the phone, I looked again at the number, and at the top of that scrap of paper I wrote "John."

MORPHOLOGY, VISUALIZATION, AND PRAYER

W ithin a week of my miracle-inspired decision to meet the healer, I was seated in the waiting room of John's office on the Upper East Side of Manhattan. I learned much later that I would likely not have gotten an appointment so quickly if I had not mentioned that I learned about John through George. I was a little nervous about this meeting. What would it be like? What was going to happen? Who was this guy that called himself a healer? I was still doubtful that John had any legitimate skills or abilities and considered the possibility that he could be a rather odd fellow. It did not help at all that John booked his first session with new clients for two hours. What were we going to do for two hours? It also didn't help that John's waiting room was not exactly what I was expecting. The area was long and narrow, more like a waiting hallway than a room. There was an odd mix of seating choices that didn't match at all: a wooden bench with spindle back, a small two-seated couch, an armchair, and a couple of other small chairs. I came to realize that the multiple doors that opened into this waiting hallway were separate offices unrelated at all to John. There was a psychologist, a psychiatrist, and a neurologist. John just rented one office at the end of the waiting area which was right next to the bathroom. It was a bit of a relief when I determined several minutes later that none of the people seated in the space were waiting for John, just me. I was next. It also struck me that there was no receptionist. I didn't know exactly what to do when I arrived. I looked around, and nobody else seemed to mind that there was no way for me to announce my arrival, so I sat down. It wasn't until the next person walked in a few minutes later and sat down without announcing herself that I was sure that I had made a proper entrance. I sat and assumed that John the healer would eventually come looking for me.

Before I tell you about that first two-hour encounter with John, I will tell you a little more about him and what he does. I have come to know John to be a kind and friendly soul. He has encountered a lot of people with a wide variety of physical, social, and psychological challenges, and I find that he approaches his clients with calm and cool empathy. It is easy to trust John. That's not to say that he is some kind of mild-mannered pushover nor is he an incense burning soothsayer. On the contrary, John is an outspoken realist with a zest for life. Now in his sixties, John spent his younger adult life running a private business manufacturing dental implants. He has a keen sense of business and a no-nonsense attitude and approach. That demeanor permeates all that he does and makes him very different from the stereotypical "Bob Newhart" type counselor or advisor. Which leads me to what exactly it is that John does.

John is not a psychologist, psychiatrist, or medical doctor. He has formal training in what he does, but none of them qualify him to be called doctor in any way. Now, I am not an expert in all that John does, but I will attempt to summarize here the ways that John has worked with me. John has taught me that the cancer that I am battling was brought upon by my own behaviors. I will explain that further a little later in this chapter. A primary goal of my work with him is to learn how to alter those behaviors and so effect the progress of the disease. How? *Morphology and counseling* and *visualization*. In addition to teaching me to alter my behavior, John *heals,* plain and simple. I will delve into each of these three techniques in a little more detail; remember, I am sharing my experiences working with John. I am not an expert in any of these techniques. There is plenty of information on the internet if you want a more comprehensive study of any of these practices.

Morphology is an ancient art and science which categorizes virtually every element of the human face and correlates the size and shape of each of these facial features to specific qualities of a person's personality and temperament. Sounds crazy at first, but morphology is commonly studied and practiced today to assess team dynamics, improve outcomes of sales efforts, and much more. John has combined what he quickly observed about my personality and temperament with the behaviors that cause RCC and has counseled me on how to manage my temperament and change my behavior to affect the progression of my disease. I will go into this further as this chapter unfolds, but remember that I alluded to you in chapter 1 that these techniques have absolutely improved my relationship with April, Christina, and Madeline. If for no other reason, the improved quality of these relationships alone has made every minute of time I have spent with John well worth the effort.

Visualization has been a significant element of my work with John. Through visualization, I have learned to alter my behaviors and heal myself. Sometimes visualizations are basic and logical like picturing the tumors that are in my lungs and seeing them shrink or cleaning them away with brooms or shovels. Sometimes visualizations are a bit more abstract like picturing a person or situation that causes a negative response or behavior and compelling myself in my mind to behave differently or to separate myself from the stimulus by walking away or even crossing a bridge. As odd as this may seem, I have altered my own behavior and even seen the results of certain medical tests become altered over time after repeating certain visualizations. I will explain this in further detail later in this chapter.

Finally, plain and simple, John heals. He channels energy through his hands into my body and causes my ailments to go away. It is prayer. John heals through prayer, through God. As he described it to me, "I am a vessel. God is the healer." I am sure there are plenty of fakes out there willing to take your money and claim you will be healed, but I will share some of my experiences with you, and you can decide for yourself. I know this sounds difficult to believe, but it is what he does. Going back to chapter 1, if you are one of those people that believes that there is no God and you have continued to read this far into this book, please do not stop now. You can choose to believe what I am describing to you or not, but I have plenty more to share with you and you have come too far to stop now!

Back to my first visit with John. As I sat in that skinny waiting area wondering who John was and when he would appear to call me in, I knew nothing of morphology, healing, or visualizations. I was still wondering what this "healer" would do and was skeptical that any of it would work for me. About five minutes past my scheduled appointment time, a woman came out of the office door near the bathroom. His last client? It was the right guess because a minute later a man appeared, and looking down the long thin space he questioned into the air, "Frank?" I got up and followed him into his office. My immediate impression was that I did not dislike him. John is around five feet and eight inches tall, with an average build, salt-and-pepper hair brushed straight back, a pleasant smile, and a calm but confident voice. He has a disarming demeanor that put me right at ease. His office was amply sized, but I found it odd that it was scantily furnished with a small desk and chair, a lounge chair, a couch, and a small armchair right next to the desk. That is where I sat. The office was barely decorated. After we exchanged some pleasantries and completed some paperwork, we got right down to the business of the next two hours.

That first session with John went by rather quickly. I can't honestly say that I remember all that we talked about during our two-hour session, but I was guarded. I wanted to make sure that I would not give him information about me or my personal life that he could somehow use to lead me to believe that he was obtaining insights about me that I had simply shared with him moments before. Still, we covered a fair bit of ground in that first session. I shared the details of my physical history, including my diagnosis of renal cell carcinoma, my surgery and post-surgical care, and the current status of my condition. I told him how many years I was married and the names and ages of my two daughters. John shared background on the services that he provides, including education on morphology. I had never heard of it before, and it was interesting to learn that it is a centuries-old practice that carries a degree of credibility even though its efficacy is a somewhat controversial topic in the scientific and clinical communities.

John applied his principles of morphology to me. He explained to me that there are four basic facial types, each carrying a unique and specific set of personality traits that you could expect to be exhibited by a person presenting with those particular facial features. The four facial types exist on a continuum. In essence, any particular face could present with features from more than one of the facial types, and so the individual would exhibit personality traits representing a blend of two or more of the four basic types. Again, I am not an expert in facial morphology, and the interested reader could easily do a web search on the topic to learn more.

John informed me that I predominantly exhibit facial features to categorize me in the bilious type. The primary characteristics associated with the bilious temperament are consistent with that of a strong-willed nature. The bilious are conquerors, dominant, domineering, and bossy. They persist tirelessly. In short, as John further described it, I am a "type A" personality with a strong desire to succeed and a tireless drive to achieve my personal goals. I found it interesting that he was able to type me in a way that I thought to be rather accurate. At the same time, it was by now 8:00 p.m. on a weeknight, and I was in my suit and tie, having finished a ten-plus hour day in my leadership role at the hospital. So either morphology worked or John chose to start his "show" with a pretty good educated guess. I wasn't sure yet.

John explained to me further the ramifications of my bilious personality type. Because of my desire to succeed at my personal goals that, by my nature, I set at a high level, combined with my controlling nature, I worry. I worry about success. I worry about failure. I worry about what might happen tomorrow or next week or next year that will get in my way of my success. I obsess about the unknown, and I solve problems before they happen. He explained that this was a problem for me as I battle renal cell carcinoma because worry and stress can contribute to the progression of the disease. He would work with me and teach me to live for today and not worry as much about tomorrow. Now this visit with John was becoming rather intriguing. He was exactly right about my obsessive focus on the future, and Dr. Mike told me after my surgery that stress was bad for my condition. This linkage between John's observations and Dr. Mike's clinical advice impressed me.

John continued to analyze my tendency to worry. He looked at me in silence for a moment and then told me that I worry about my children too much. I did not find that to be particularly profound on its surface. He knew I had two single daughters who were at the time aged twenty and twenty-two. Who wouldn't worry? What happened next was fascinating to me. He looked at a picture of my two daughters. Based upon their morphology, he told me things about their personalities and was incredibly specific about the things that I worry about as relates to each of them. I was amazed. He spoke about them as if he knew them for years, as if he personally had experienced my daughters' very behaviors that caused me to worry. Now, they are both great people, and none of John's observations were of an embarrassing nature. Still, he was so specific and so descriptive of their individual personalities and behavior traits that it would be unfair to Christina and Madeline for me to explain further. I was becoming quickly convinced that there was something to this morphology while at the same time, John was beginning to form his plan for how he would council and teach me to worry less and reduce the stress that I bring upon myself.

John shifted our discussion to the nature of the condition that I was battling and the nature of disease and afflictions in general. He explained to me that every physical condition that we experience—from a minor backache to a heart condition to advanced cancer and everything in between—we bring upon ourselves through our temperament and behaviors. Since we bring them upon ourselves, we have the power to control their progression and even reverse their effects. He further explained to me that ailments of the kidney are brought upon by anger. He told me that I was an angry person by nature, and that fact, combined with my struggles to control that anger, has resulted in my diagnosis. I had a hard time relating to this entire discussion. I viewed myself as a nice person. I went out of my way to help others. I was empathetic and had always attributed my ability to lead large numbers of staff to my behaviors that included recognizing good performance, not overreacting to mistakes, and creating a light and friendly environment in the workplace. Sure, I set high expectations and demanded superior performance, but I rarely lost my temper and never yelled at or demeaned my staff. I remember thinking that John had missed his mark on this one.

When I arrived home, April was anxious to hear about my first session, and I was eager to tell her. She was intrigued by John's observations from the morphology segment of our session and was amazed by John's observations about our daughters. She asked me several times, and I assured her each time that I shared nothing about our family that would have given John even a hint about our daughters' personalities. Then I told April about John's hypothesis that I had brought upon myself the RCC. I told her how John had missed the mark, how he concluded that my own anger caused my condition. After all, I am not an angry person by nature. Huh. April looked at me for a minute with a bewildered puppy dog face. I realized later that she was wondering if I was kidding and was waiting for me to start laughing. When I returned her gaze with an equally confused expression, she just started to laugh. Really laugh. "You don't think you are an angry person?" She sort of asked it as a question, but it was more of a bewildered realization on her part. She continued, "You had to go to a healer to tell you that you are angry? Of course you are angry. You get mad at everything. You get mad at what you see on the news. You get mad when the girls don't act the way you think they should. You get mad when the house is messy. You even get mad when people don't agree with you." The list went on. This all correlated exactly with what John had described to me. It turned out that he was right, and I had some work to do. I came to believe at that moment that if I was going to live, I needed to control my stress, worry less, and figure out how to stop allowing things that happen around me, over which I have no control, from making me angry.

I visited John again two weeks later and began to learn how I would alter and control these traits that were having a negative impact on my life. I had come to realize that these traits were not only causing my illness but were also affecting my relationship with the people that were most important in my life. John explained to me that I would not be able to eliminate from my personality the attributes I did not want; in a way they are hardwired into who I am. However, it is possible to manage those attributes by recognizing how they manifest and consciously changing my response.

Now, I have seen my share of situation comedies that have made fun of their characters as they tried to alter their behavior and their response to outside stimuli, but I was willing to give it a try. During this visit and for many visits after, John and I discussed the kinds of things that made me angry, the things that I worry about, and how I worry. I came to appreciate that much more of what I encounter each day is out of my control than is actually within my control. I needed to focus on the things I could control. Appreciating, however, is far different than doing. How would I alter my responses to outside stimuli? John introduced me to visualization. After first relaxing and taking some deliberate breaths, I would visually play in my mind a scenario, usually one that would normally cause me to become angry or worrisome. Then, I would see myself responding to that negative stimulus in a way that I would prefer to act. I would repeat that visualization a minimum of twice per day for some number of weeks or months. Eventually, that negative stimulus would no longer elicit the negative response that it once did.

There are other types of visualization that John taught me. I have visualized myself manually cleaning my lungs, sweeping or shoveling or shrinking the tumors that were growing within them. I learned to use visualization to manage a variety of physical conditions. One example was the measure of my kidney function. At one point, my creatinine levels—a measure of the function of my one remaining kidney—were on the rise. This was an anticipated side effect of the medication I was taking, but for some reason three monthly blood tests in a row had indicated marked elevation. To give you the context, two healthy kidneys would produce a creatinine level of 1.0, a healthy baseline. Each time the creatinine level doubles, kidney function is halved. So a creatinine level of 2.0 would indicate 50 percent kidney function. After the removal of my left kidney, my baseline creatinine level was approximately 1.4, a good function for one kidney which will often do extra duty when the other is lost. As a side effect of my medication, my creatinine levels were running between 1.6 and 1.8, and my doctors were comfortable that this was a safe range for my age and condition. For these particular three blood tests I have referenced, my creatinine levels ranged between 1.9 and 2.1, a level that still did not seem to concern my doctors but a trend that did not make me the slightest bit happy. I knew the importance of hydration to kidney function, and during this three-month period of upward trending creatinine I made sure that I was well hydrated. I also made sure that I made no changes to my diet that could affect these test results. John gave me a visualization that had helped others control their kidney function. The details of the visualization have no logical relationship to the kidney, so I won't describe it here. I repeated that visualization twice daily for the subsequent month. At my next blood test, my creatine had returned to 1.7. Since then, my creatinine levels have been running in the range of 1.4 to 1.5, my premedication baseline, even though I continue to take the same medication that had driven those levels up into the range of 2.0+. Dr. Tom, my oncologist, remarked on the reduction in the trend yet no doctor has been able to explain to me why the range had come down. I continue to this day doing any multiple sets of daily visualizations.

I want to pause here to make two points about my work with John. This work is in no way a replacement for western medicine. I go to my doctor every three weeks, I get blood work every month, I get scans every three months, and I do everything that my doctors recommend. John even incorporates my clinical treatments into my visualizations. I think of my work with John as a complement to my clinical treatments. Also, about six months after I began working with John, April had some news for me that she delivered with a big smile. After a day-long visit we had with Christina and Madeline, April told me that our daughters wanted to know what she did with their old dad. Their new dad was easier to talk to and more enjoyable to be around. They had no idea that I was working to change my responses to outside stimuli that caused me worry, stress, and anger, but they remarked about the result. So you see, my work with John impacted my life in ways that went well beyond the physical ailments I originally met him to address.

There is another very important component to my work with John, arguably the component most difficult for me to explain and for you to understand. I continue to work with John once per week for one hour per session. A significant portion of every visit is devoted to healing. John channels energy through his hands into my body, and that energy heals. He places his hands over the area of my body that requires healing, on most days focusing primarily on my lungs. He does not touch me; his hands are usually six to eight inches away from my skin. Still, I can feel the heat from the energy penetrating my body. Sometimes the energy is so intense that it feels like there is a heating pad on my chest. John has explained to me that this is not his energy; he really does not do much at all. This is God's energy channeling through John into my body. I know this sounds too crazy to believe, so you must be wondering how it is that I am even telling you about it.

Remember that I made that first visit to John out of desperation. My first treatment had not worked, and my tumor growth was clinically remarkable. I had just been placed on an oral chemotherapy which provided greater hope, but a different kind of hope than that first treatment. My hope was that this new treatment would stop the progress of my condition, slowing or stopping the growth of the tumors, and work for approximately nine months, when I would switch to another treatment. Three or so months after my first visit to John, it was time for me to get a scan of my lungs to determine if my new treatment was working. On my last visit to John before my scan, he told me that he was sure that the tumors had not grown, and he was fairly certain that they were smaller than they were at the time of my last scan. I thought that was a bold statement; he knew the progression of RCC as well as I did.

I was nervous on the day of my scan. When the scan was done, I drove home. While I was still driving, I received a call from Dr. Abe, my oncologist at the time. In his exact words, this was a "wow scan." He reminded me that our hope was that the tumors had not grown since my last scan. In fact, not only had they not grown, but they had shrunk in size to a degree that was "remarkable." There was that word again, only this time it was in my favor. Some of the tumors were half the size that they were at my last scan, and some of the smaller ones that had newly appeared at my last scan were now gone. To be fair, I was not the first person this had ever happened to; there were documented cases where tumor sizes were reduced with these medications. Still, this was not the norm. I continued my work with John. While this particular drug is effective for, on average, nine months, I remained on that drug approximately three years before I had to make a change. During that time, my tumors did not ever grow, and no new tumors ever appeared. A number of smaller tumors disappeared over that three-year period.

To this day, I continue to work with John for one hour every week. My quality of life has improved, and my relationship with April, Christina, Madeline and so many of my closest family and friends has been greatly enhanced. There are so many reasons why my sessions with John continue to be an important part of my life.

- My time with John is a consistent reinforcement of the lessons I have learned to reduce and manage anger, stress, and worry in my life.
- My quality of life and relationship with those that I love continues to be improve.
- I continue to utilize new visualization techniques to manage ongoing and new challenges.
- Progression of the RCC has slowed to a near halt for five years.
- John has used God's healing energy to resolve other physical ailments I have encountered during the time that I have known him.

This last point is worth some further explanation through a couple of examples.

During one of my visits with John, I was sitting on his couch. He stopped our session and asked me if my back was hurting. I was having some lower back pain, but that was normal for me. Whenever I sat on a couch, as opposed to a hardbacked chair, I would experience lower back discomfort. I wasn't sure how John knew that I was beginning to experience that pain, but he was right. He told me that he could fix that pain for me and asked me to stand up. He stood behind me, and though I could not watch him work, he assured me that he was not going to touch me. I felt a sensation as if John leaned gently on the middle of my back and followed my spine down to its base. The sensation started again in the middle of my back, but this time I felt light pressure as the sensation moved down to the base of my spine. He informed me that my coccyx bone—my tail bone—was out of alignment. Once again, I felt light pressure, but this time on my tailbone; and that sensation shifted toward the right side of my waist. This happened several times. John only held his hands over my back; he never touched me. When he was done, John told me that I would no longer experience pain. He was right. I sat back on the couch and have sat on many dozens of couches and soft chairs since then, and I have never experienced that lower back pain again.

One of the several side effects of my chemotherapy medication is a phenomenon called hand-foot syndrome. It is a temporary condition that causes intense pain in the palms and fingers and in the heels and balls of the feet. The areas effected become extremely sensitive to touch, making walking and use of the hands difficult and painful. Normally when I experienced the syndrome, I would speak with Dr. Tom and stop taking the medication. After just a couple of days, the pain would disappear. On one of my visits, when the pain was very uncomfortable, I explained the condition to John. I sat on his couch with my feet elevated, and he placed his hands over the tops and bottoms of my feet. The heat I felt right through my shoes was intense. After about ten minutes I stood up, and the pain was greatly reduced. I was able to walk back to my car with only a small amount of discomfort, and by the next morning, the pain was gone without ever stopping the medication. Now, whenever the pain coincides with a visit to John's office, he works on my feet, and in almost every instance the pain is relieved by the next morning.

I have been blessed to have met John. Before I describe to you the most special event that has ever happened in my life, I will pause briefly in the next short chapter to summarize the miracle-inspired decisions that took me on my path to my good friend John.

SECOND PATH

In the last three chapters, I described to you the path that I followed in my personal life—the path that led me to John. Meeting John was a genuine blessing. For the nearly six years since my diagnosis and surgery, I have lived an active and normal life, due in no small part to John's ability to deliver God's healing. As I have described in some detail, my experience with John has brought me more than physical well-being; it has changed the way I think about and work with the people that I encounter every day, and it has greatly improved my relationship with the people who are the closest to me.

My path to John was simple but nonetheless inspired by God's manipulation of time and events.

A home in the country. It started with April and my desire to have a weekend getaway in the country. A friend of ours told us about a development in Pennsylvania that looked to have all of the amenities and recreational activities that we were looking for, including golf and skiing, right within the gates of the development. After careful consideration, we purchased two lots and lined up a builder. This was a meaningful investment for us, and we took these decisions very seriously. We believed that we were well on our path to achieving our objective; it all felt very right. Until we met the builder. What was supposed to be a milestone day when we would begin the process of building our new home turned into an eye-opening session with a total stranger who completely changed our views about the very place we had selected and made our investments—both financial and emotional. We were all in until the miracle that happened in that hotel great room and our resulting decision to abandon our plans to build in Evergreen Ridge and search for a new area to purchase our second home. Saugerties was a natural place for us to spend the next ski season or two. We never expected that Saugerties would be the place we would select for our weekend getaways, nor did we ever expect to meet George who referred me to his friend John. None of that would have happened—none of it could have happened—if we had not had our meeting with Joe, the contractor who shared the reasons why we might *not* want to build in Evergreen Ridge.

Morphology, Visualization, and Prayer. I would have never foreseen myself ever spending time with a healer. I did not believe such people were credible, and if there was one that was genuine, I never considered the possibility that I could be the beneficiary of his or her abilities. There are a lot of fakes out there, taking advantage of people when they are most vulnerable. Voodoo medicine, I thought. Not for me. Not for anyone who was logical and intelligent. But things were not going my way at the time. My rather difficult treatment was not working, my tumors were growing, and I was about to begin my medical journey again from square one. A new oncologist and a new treatment. I did not know that this new treatment was going to work. I was afraid that it would not. Then those words from April that ring in my ears to this day, "What do you have to lose?" At that moment, I made the miracle-inspired decision to act against all that made sense to me, to go against what I thought was my better judgment and spend money and time with a healer. That was one of the best and most important decisions I have made in my life. I made it, once again, because God manipulated time and events, and April uttered those simple words: "What do you have to lose?"

I have now shared with you six miracle-inspired decisions that led me down two parallel paths: one in my professional life and one in my personal life. The journey down these paths prepared me for the most difficult challenge I have ever had to face and concurrently taught me to live my life in a more fulfilling and satisfactory way. The past nearly six years have been some of the best years of my life. How many people have you ever heard say that after receiving a life-threatening cancer diagnosis?

I often wonder how many other times my decisions were miracle inspired and how many other paths I was traveling that were concurrent to the two that I have described. I don't know. I suspect that there were more. What about you? Have you ever experienced a miracle? Can you think of decisions you have made during the course of your life that prepared *you* for future challenges…that possibly saved *your* life? If you have never experienced a miracle…*are you looking hard enough?*

I hope what I have shared so far has caused you to consider the paths you have traveled in your life and to consider the paths that might be ahead. I also hope that what remains to be told in these pages further inspire you to consider the possibilities.

SIMPLY BEAUTIFUL

I was visiting John one Wednesday evening. It was the fall of 2017. I was sitting in the armchair right next to his desk; he was seated in his desk chair facing me with his hands extended over my chest. This was a typical scene whenever I visited John, and he and I had and continue to have a standing appointment: Wednesday night at six-thirty. Almost every Wednesday night.

After working with John for over four years, our visits now have a relatively consistent format. We have become friends, so we usually start with five or ten minutes of small talk, catching up on the events of the week since we last visited. Sometimes we talk about work, and sometimes we talk about family or friends. John is a new grandfather, and he often shares some recent pictures of his beautiful granddaughter. That casual discussion usually gravitates to a slightly more serious discussion about my work life. John continually reinforces the lessons that I have learned. Managing stress and anger is a life journey, and John knows that work is a great source of both for me. Sometimes he senses that I have had a tough day or couple of days since our last visit. We talk about those difficult moments and reinforce the techniques I have learned to release the stress…don't worry about what I can't control…new visualizations…getting angry does not solve anything. The remainder of our time together is spent healing. John extends his hands over my body, most often my chest, and I experience the healing power. Sometimes I feel heat radiating into the area of my body beneath his hands. Sometimes the heat is intense, as if a heating pad is resting against my body. When the heat is that intense, I still look down to see that John's hands are not even touching the area being affected. As usual, they are six to eight inches away from my body. I still find it to be amazing. Sometimes I feel vibrations in my chest. It's a rumbling feeling that startled me the first couple of times I felt it. Now it's just normal. When the vibrations are strong, John usually asks, "Do you feel that?" When I tell him I do, he replies, "Yeah, I do too." When I have pain someplace like my feet or my back, John devotes a portion of that hour extending his hands over that area that is in pain. Almost always, my pain is relieved.

This particular Wednesday night in the fall of 2017 started like every other. We were about half the way through the session, and John had his hands extended over my chest. Sometimes we continue our small talk during the healing, but this particular time we were both quiet. I was resting with my eyes closed. John was doing his thing. It was John that broke the silence. "God wants me to show you how He works." John gets feelings that are messages all the time. He explained that it was not a voice or anything that is spoken to him. He just senses it. I knew John well enough that I was not startled and trusted that whatever he was going to do would only be in my best interest. So I just said, "Okay." He stood up and dimmed the light in the room. The room was still lit well enough to be able to see just fine. John told me that when he has done this in the past, his clients have seen a halo over his head and that it is easier to see the halo when the lights are dimmed. Again, my unemotional response was "Okay." He then walked in front of me, and we held hands. He told me that he was going to pray, and he asked me to focus on the center of his forehead. I obliged.

John closed his eyes, and with absolutely no expression on his face, he became completely quiet. He swayed ever so gently left to right and left again as we faced each other, holding hands. He was standing in front of me while I sat in the same chair I sat in during every visit. I focused quietly on his forehead. What happened next is the most incredible and special thing that has ever happened to me, something I have recalled joyfully every single day since and I am sure I will continue to recall every day for the rest of my life.

John's face began to change. His cheekbones became higher, and his cheeks became narrowed. His narrowed cheeks came to a small point under his mouth, forming a new chin where a small rounded chin used to exist. His mouth became smaller, and his pursed lips formed a pleasant and easy smile. His eyes became smaller, his skin became perfectly smooth, and his hair became more flattened and pushed directly back as if it were tucked neatly under a veil. The transformation was somewhat like the action that takes place in Michael Jackson's music video for the song titled "Black or White." He was no longer John. I knew that I was looking at Mary. I was looking at our Blessed Mother.

Now, most of us have played that game where you stare at yourself intently in the mirror and your own facial features start to change. If you have never done it, you should try. Stare intensely at a single facial feature in the mirror. Don't blink and don't move your eyes from that feature you selected. After a minute or so, you don't look like yourself. You look distorted. You look different. Do you know how you end the game? You blink. As soon as you blink, you look like your old self again. As I stared at the face that I knew was our Blessed Mother, I had the presence of mind to wonder if that was what was happening to me. So like I did when I played that game in the mirror as a child, I blinked. The image of Mary disappeared, and John's face returned. But without refocusing on John's forehead, the image of Mary's face returned within a few seconds with her sweet smile and perfect complexion. I squinted, and I could see John's face. It seemed to be behind Mary's face. The image of Mary did not disappear this time. I relaxed my eyes and blinked again, and the image of Mary was its clearest. I was mesmerized.

She is beautiful. Not like our stereotype of beauty in modern America. She was simply beautiful. Her small eyes were reminiscent of a woman's eyes with no makeup or eye shadow; but the skin and area around her eyes were perfect, devoid of the marks and shadows most women seek to cover with the very makeup that makes their eyes look bigger and sometimes brighter. I kept looking at her smile. It was pleasant; her lips were together, so I could not see her teeth. Her mouth was small, and her smile was so slight that it caused no creases in her cheeks, yet I knew from her smile that She loves me very much. I don't know how long She was present with me, but for some time I forgot that Her presence was in the same place that John used to stand. I could feel that I was smiling back at Her. I was calm and happy and so very satisfied to be in Her presence. I did not want that moment to end.

Mary continued to gently sway left to right and back again, just like John was doing. I cannot tell you what She was wearing or even if Her body was dressed in John's clothes. I was so enamored by Her face that I never stopped looking at it. The room remained dim, but as Mary swayed left to right, an intensely white light started to show from behind Her neck. It was almost as if the light was trying to hide behind Mary. When She gently shifted to the right, the light appeared from Her left and then disappeared behind Her. When Mary shifted gently to the left the light appeared again, this time from Her right, and then disappeared behind Her again. This happened over and over and over again. The light was whiter than the whitest light bulb I have ever seen. It was brighter than the sun. Yet as white and bright and pure as the light was, I was able to look right into it as it appeared from behind Mary's neck, and I did not need to squint, and the light did not hurt my eyes. I was having a great time; it was euphoric. I did not want it to end. I was not scared; I was not wondering at all what was happening or why this was happening. I didn't care about any of that. If someone told me that the whole experience lasted thirty seconds or that it lasted thirty minutes, I would believe either. Time seemed not to exist as long as I was in Her presence. It was magical. I never experienced anything like it before or since. Unless I am blessed to be visited by Mary again, I am quite sure that I will never again experience the simple bliss that I felt while in Her presence—at least not in this lifetime.

As suddenly as the bright light began to appear, it ceased to show itself from behind Mary's neck as She continued to gently sway left to right and back again. Just as in Michael Jackson's video, only in slow motion, Mary's simple beauty turned back into John's familiar face. His eyes were still closed. He was still in prayer. As if he knew that Mary had left my presence, John let go of my hands and took a step away from me. As if I had not seen enough glory, a halo appeared over John's head. It was not like a halo you would see on an angel in a child's school play. It did not sit high over his head. It seemed to emanate from behind his head. It extended in a perfect circle over his head. While the inner and outer edges of the ring were well-defined, the halo itself was comprised of a smoky light. It was almost as if a flashlight was shining through a fog, yet the inner and outer edges of the ring were sharp. Again, I can't tell you if I was seeing that halo for thirty seconds or for thirty minutes. Time still had no meaning. Then John opened his eyes, and the halo slowly faded away, as did my feeling of euphoria. The experience was ended.

I explained to John what I had seen. This was not the first time that our Blessed Mother had appeared to one of his clients. We were both humbled and so very happy. I asked about the light. John explained that the light was an archangel, there to protect me. That raised a lot of questions in my mind. Why would I need protection during the very time that the Blessed Mother was visiting me? Why couldn't She protect me? I didn't ask. It didn't matter. The experience was so real and so personal and so beautiful that no questions mattered to me. As I mentioned earlier, this was an experience that I have recalled happily every single day—literally every single day—since it happened. I strive to pray daily, and as part of those prayers I thank Her every day for our visit.

It was after that experience that I began to wonder why She chose me to visit. Why then? I had been seeing John for nearly five years. Those thoughts turned into a sense of amazement that I even came to meet John, a healer. Voodoo medicine; that is what I used to think of people who were healers. I thought about John and how he was introduced to me by George. I thought how lucky I was to have met George. I thought how lucky I was that Joe the contractor seemed to convince us not to build in Evergreen Ridge, or I would have never met George. I thought how lucky I was to be alive and how lucky it was that I joined Northwell so I could meet Dr. Mike. I thought how lucky I was to have been able to get comfortable inside of the ORs before I had to go into one for my own rather complex surgery. How lucky…how lucky…how lucky…

Then I realized that I was not lucky at all. There is no such thing as luck. I realized that God had been inspiring me to make the decisions I needed to make so that I would end up at Northwell, so that I would end up at Lenox Hill, so that I would end up in Saugerties, so that I would meet George who would introduce me to John. There is no such thing as luck. I was open enough to the divine influences of God to make decisions that were counterintuitive to me, decisions that I would not normally have made, decisions that I didn't even know why I made at the time that I made them. I pieced together my miracle-inspired career path. I pieced together my miracle-inspired personal path. Once I pieced them together, they hit me like a brick on the side of my head. How could I have not realized this miraculous path was unfolding as it was happening? How could I have thought these were all coincidences? I don't know how that could be, but once I pieced them together they changed my view of how much God actually loves us all. It gave incredibly new meaning to the story of the footprints in the sand. "I would never leave you. During your times of trial and suffering, when you see only one set of footprints, it was then that I carried you." If you don't know the whole story, you should search it on the internet. Once I pieced them together, I had new hope and understanding about my future and the paths that I will journey going forward; and once I pieced them together, I knew I needed to write it all down because I knew there must be others who have not yet pieced together their own lifetime of miracle-inspired decisions.

Please get busy. You have a lot to think about. You have a lot to piece together. God loves you as much as He loves me. You have made miracle-inspired decisions, and you have miracle-inspired decisions in your future. We all do.

TRUST AND HOPE

I am finally able to share with you the most important lesson I have learned from all the experiences I have shared throughout these chapters. It is THE message I was compelled to deliver the moment I decided that I had to write this book.

I have a new trust in God and renewed hope for my future.

For sure, that trust is not perfect, and I have my moments where I have concerns and doubts. I am not proud of those moments, but I suppose they happen to us all because we are, after all, only human. Still, my trust is stronger than ever, and my hope springs eternal. Now, even after I pieced together my miracle-inspired life paths, I did not recognize this trust and hope that resided within me. I didn't realize it was there until another event that occurred in my life, an event that occurred only weeks before I started writing this book.

As you now know, the RCC that invaded my body had already metastasized to my lungs at the time of my diagnosis. I mentioned in chapter 1 that it had later metastasized to my brain. What I did not tell you is that the brain tumor was found in February of 2018. It was found while I was creating the outline for this book and just a couple of weeks before I wrote its first words. I continued my writing without any pause as I was confident that its messages would not change.

It was a cold and snowy February 2018. I was experiencing some new symptoms which I assumed were side effects from my medication. In fact, the nausea, dry heaves, and headaches I was experiencing were all explained on the web as side effects of my current treatment. Still, when I explained what was happening, Dr. Tom ordered a brain MRI. "I don't expect to find anything unusual, but let's rule out any metastasis. Then I'll send you to a GI specialist, and we'll find out what's going on with your stomach."

The MRI revealed a small tumor in the back of my brain. It was around a quarter of an inch in diameter. Still, a tumor in the brain is a tumor in the brain, so we acted quickly. I was referred to the department of radiation medicine and scheduled for gamma knife treatment. Gamma knife does not involve a knife at all. It is the delivery of high intensity radiation targeted to destroy the tumor in a single treatment. April and I drove together to the treatment center on the back end of a nor'easter, one cold and windy March morning. The entire process was completed in just a few hours, just enough time for the storm to finally end and the sun to begin to shine. The actual radiation treatment took ten minutes. As the doctors expected, my follow-up MRI a couple of months later confirmed that the tumor had been destroyed. What remains is a hollow shell, and the doctors expect it to shrink to a small scar in the coming months. But that is not why I am telling you this story.

When I went for that follow-up MRI, the neurosurgeon that was caring for me, Dr. Michael, asked, "Why did you go for the MRI that detected this tumor?" I explained to him my symptoms and the recommendation from Dr. Tom that I have the test. He responded, "You're lucky. The symptoms you were experiencing were not caused by this tumor. The tumor was too small and not in a spot that would cause those symptoms." I found Dr. Michael's observations intriguing, because the nausea, dry heaves, and headaches stopped the day that Dr. Tom ordered the MRI even though a couple of weeks went by before I actually received the treatment. Now, I have already explained what I think about "luck." No such thing. Decide for yourself how it is and why it is that I had those symptoms and Dr. Tom recommended that test because this is also not the reason I am telling you this story.

The reason I am telling you this story is because from the moment that Dr. Tom told me that the MRI had revealed a brain tumor to the time that Dr. Michael told me that it was dead, I was not afraid, concerned, or distracted. I not only continued to plan the writing of this book, but I continued to work with little interruption, and I continued my personal life with no disruption. I was not even anxious when it was time for the follow-up MRI. I slept just fine the night before that test and woke up and got ready to leave the house like it was any other day. Don't get me wrong; I did not know what the results of that test would be, and I had considered the possibility that this tumor or related complications could be the beginning of the end of my life. The doctors were calm and confident, and they assured me that this tumor was not life threatening. But a brain tumor is still a brain tumor. My brain is now imaged every three months because even the doctors cannot assure me that my brain will remain tumor free.

I remained calm because I knew I was not alone. I knew that I would be inspired to make the right decisions, and I was confident that—whatever the outcome—God would be by my side to help me through whatever was coming my way. I had developed a trust whose strength I had not known. I never wavered in my hope for the joy and happiness that would continue after this event was behind me. If what was coming my way was the beginning of my end, then so be it. It will happen to us all at some point. But I knew that I was not experiencing this challenge in isolation. Whatever was to happen, it was going to be okay; it was going to be right. I was not afraid.

When you come to recognize your own miracle-inspired decisions, then you too will build greater trust, and you too will learn eternal hope. As I have already urged you, please get busy. You have a lot to think about. You have a lot to piece together. God loves you as much as He loves me. You have made miracle-inspired decisions, and you have miracle-inspired decisions in your future. We all do.

REFLECTIONS

Free will is possibly one of the most complicating factors in our lives. I never thought about it that way before. I have always understood that we all have free will since my religion classes in grade school. We residents of the United States don't always call it free will; sometimes we call it our freedom. In fact, freedom of choice is sometimes included in the very definition of free will. Whether you believe that these freedoms were granted by your God or by your country, it is difficult to argue that every human has the ability to make choices. Even those that reside in countries with less freedom than the United States, all people have the freedom to follow the rules or to not follow the rules. Free will resides in each and every one of us, but free will makes our lives complicated. We don't know what the future holds. We do not understand the ramifications of the decisions we make freely every day of our lives. Many of us, I am sure, have experienced a situation where we concluded that we would have made a different decision had we only known the ultimate outcome of that decision. I know that I have. So it is not unreasonable to conclude that free will causes us to live life in insolation; we feel alone and vulnerable when we have to make big decisions. Life would be easier if we did not need to make difficult decisions; it would be better if we did not have to live with the results of the decision we make without the benefit of a full understanding of their ramifications at the time we have to make the decision. To complicate things even further, every single person around us is making decisions, utilizing their own free will, and those decisions can so easily derail a sound decision that we have made. I think of this as decision collisions, and they are the direct result of tens of millions of people living on the face of the earth, each utilizing their own free will to make decisions. What a chaotic and random world we live in. How much simpler and easier and less punishing would our world be if we were not granted this right, this "gift" that we call free will. Right? Well, not really. Not from my perspective.

Life is certainly more uncertain, more complicated, and more difficult at times because we have the right to make decisions, and then we are required to live the results of those decisions; but our free will also allows us to create our futures, explore possibilities that might otherwise be closed to us, and obtain wonderful life achievements that might otherwise be completely out of our reach. As a result of my six miracle-inspired decisions, I have also come to the conclusion that I have not lived my life in isolation. If you take nothing else from this book, please consider the following learnings that I have drawn from the path my life has taken:

First, *I have not walked through this life alone.* I made each of my miracle-inspired decisions utilizing my own free will. I, of course, made many of those decisions together with April, but together we were not coerced into making any one of those decisions. We were never even made to feel threatened or forced into those decisions by the many decisions being made around us by others utilizing their own free will. We were, however, influenced, even manipulated into making those decisions. We were influenced and manipulated by the timing and presence of events or circumstances that caused us to make decisions that were different than we originally planned. Decisions that went counter to what we considered to be our better judgment. Decisions that I cannot fully explain even today as I look back on them. Through His manipulation of time and circumstances, I was inspired to make decisions that changed the course of my life. What a different life I would have lived if I joined another of the big 8 accounting firms and was never forced to change careers. Who knows in what industry I would have developed my expertise had I said no to Eric when he presented me with the opportunity to work in healthcare. How difficult my life would have been had I never received my preparation with Susan and later at Lenox Hill for my diagnosis, surgery, and treatment. I am fairly certain that without the counseling and healing from John, the six years since my surgery would have been filled with fear, uncertainly, and despair as compared to the trust, hope, and enriched relationship that I have with April, Madeline, and Christina, all because of the unlikely advice we received from a contractor we never met before and our decision to leave behind our six-figure investment in Evergreen Ridge (we still have not been able to sell that property) to purchase our home in Saugerties.

As I told you in chapter 1, not one of these decisions is particularly profound in and of themselves, but when linked together, they created a life path that has unquestionably helped me through the most difficult challenge in my life and made me a better and happier person. Isolation? I think not. What do you think?

Second, *however much more time I have to live on this earth, I will not finish this life alone. I have new trust in God and hope for my future.* I have become so confident that I am not alone that I face challenges in a far different manner than I have in the past. I don't profess to understand how God works. I don't know if He inspires me directly or through a guardian angel or through loved ones that have passed from this life and have earned a favored place in eternity. I am just confident that I am not alone.

When the doctors found the tumor in my brain, my reaction could easily have been disappointment and fear. It had been nearly six years since my diagnosis, and my condition was stable. No new tumors in my lungs; no new tumors anywhere. I had already outlived the odds and was hopeful that my condition would remain stable for some time to come. But neither disappointment nor fear were part of my reaction, only trust and hope. I trusted that I was well prepared to endure this next challenge, and I continued to have hope that only goodness was ahead. Goodness, however, took on a much broader definition. I recognized that even though my doctors were confident that this tumor was not life-threatening, this reactivation of the cancer could mean the beginning of my end.

Goodness now means that I am being inspired to make the best decisions possible about my treatments and about just about everything else that will come my way. Goodness means that I am not alone and never will be. Goodness means that joy and happiness reside on the other side of every difficult thing that will happen in my life. Goodness means that when it is time for me to transition from this life to the next, it will be okay. I will be ready. That is why I have eternal hope. Because I am excited about the life that I have left to live on this earth, and I am not afraid to die.

Why would I be afraid? Death will come to each and every one of us; it is not a matter of if but a matter of when. My miracle-inspired decisions—and my visit from our Blessed Mother—have proven to me that all the promises of eternal life are real. Everything I have ever learned about eternal life assures me that it is far better than our life here on earth. I am thoroughly convinced that *our best day on earth pales in comparison to the worst day we will have in heaven.* That even assumes that heaven can even have a worst day! So I have nothing to fear. Even the moment of my passing no longer worries me. I will not be alone. I will be prepared.

Are you worried about what your future holds? Are you afraid to die? Why should you be?

Third, *life is not predestined.* I needed to pay attention to the inspirations that came my way because my free will could have allowed me to make a decision other than the one I was being manipulated to make, and I would have had to live the consequences of that decision. By now, you can create the scenarios yourself. Had I not changed my mind about Evergreen Ridge, concluding for example that we had already made the property investment, I would not have purchased the home in Saugerties, would not have met John, would not have changed my relationship with my family, would not have been visited by Mary. Resist the inspiration and you go wrong; life turns out differently. Life becomes more difficult. Now, I am sure that God has inspired me more than six times, and I would be willing to bet I missed some of those inspirations. I am sure that I have made some "bad" decisions. No doctor can tell me what caused me to contract RCC; perhaps I missed some inspirations, resisted some manipulations. Perhaps those "bad" decisions caused me to become exposed to environmental factors that caused me to contract RCC. I don't know. Nobody does. It's on my list of questions to ask God when I get to heaven. I am confident that there are times that each of us turn away from God's inspiration and, for a time, send our life on a difficult path.

I wish I had the formula; I wish I knew how to read the signs and know when I am being inspired. I wish there was a way to identify those very special situations so that both you and I would never miss one again. While I do not know for sure when it is happening, I do know that in each of the six situations I have described, I had an odd feeling about the decision I was about to make. It was a funny feeling in my stomach or a nagging thought in my head that I could not shake. That feeling went away when I made the decision that I was being inspired to make. Some people might call it a sixth sense. Some people refer to it as an angel on their shoulder whispering in their ear. Some people think of it as "going with their gut." I can't tell you what it will feel like when God is inspiring you. I can't even tell you for sure when I am being inspired. All I can tell you is that when I get that funny feeling in my stomach or that nagging thought in my head, I pause and think about the decision I am about to make. I pray about it. Then I make my decision.

Consider this example.

I love to ski, and president's weekend is special at Hunter. We meet our cousin Nino and a group of his friends that weekend. We ski all day Saturday and Sunday and go out for dinner together each night. It had become a tradition. About three years ago, I was very much looking forward to president's weekend. April and I had all the arrangements made and were planning to meet up with Nino on Saturday. I woke up that Friday anticipating the long weekend as I dressed and left for work. My workday was uneventful. When I arrived home from work, I had the strangest feeling in the pit of my stomach. As the time came closer to leave for the weekend the feeling became stronger, and when I focused on the impending trip upstate the feeling became almost nauseating. Just a few minutes before it was time to leave, I told April I did not want to go. I wasn't sure why I just had an odd feeling. April does not like odd feelings, so she quickly agreed to stay home. We called Nino and told him we would be skipping the weekend.

That night it got very cold in Brooklyn. The extreme temperatures were forecasted, so we were not surprised. We learned the next morning, which was Saturday, that we had some frozen pipes on the third floor. Also not too concerning, this had happened before on cold nights, and they always thawed without consequence. On this particular Saturday, the pipes thawed around noon. This time, however, was different. A pipe had burst on the third floor. It didn't crack; it had completely separated at the point where a joint was soldered to the pipe. Water was gushing from the pipe and quickly cascaded to the second and first floors and was pooling in the basement. Since we were home, I was able to shut the water at the main almost immediately, and the damage to the two bathrooms and kitchen that were below the broken pipe was minimal. I can only imagine the amount of damage our home would have sustained if that water had run for another fifty-plus hours before we got home on Monday. We were lucky. Lucky? You know what I think about luck.

So now I pause every time I get those odd feelings, even when they are not strong or I am not even sure what I am feeling. I don't simply change my mind or make an illogical decision just because I got a strange feeling, but I pause. I think. I wonder if I am being inspired. I say a prayer. Then, I make the best decision I think I can make, and I move on.

Fourth, *I am not special. God loves you as much as He loves me, and He also knows that free will complicates your life as much as it does mine.* He is there at your side, inspiring you. All you have to do is watch and listen and feel for it. Don't resist it. Don't make rash decisions either, only to find out the next day that you just had a twenty-four-hour stomach flu! But understand that you might be receiving inspiration. Again, don't make a silly decision, but decide thoughtfully.

It would be easy to conclude that I am "one of those people" that is sensitive to messages from "the other side," someone who is able to communicate or get messages from people who have passed, able to get their guidance. Don't believe for a second that I have any abilities or senses that you or anyone else does not have. I was never "one of those people." I don't see spirits, and I don't get messages about the future. I am no different than you or anyone else, except, maybe, that I have a relationship with God. I pray every day. I talk to Him every day. I tell Him what I need, and I am open to what He wants from me. If you don't have a relationship with God, then create one. It's easy. It does not matter how old you are or how long you have lived without a relationship with Him or what things you have done that you think (or know) are bad. Pray whatever prayers you were taught as a child. If you don't remember or were never taught to pray as a child, then start tomorrow morning and every morning after by saying: "Good morning God, thanks for another day. I am here if You want me to do anything." You will be amazed how your discussion with God will expand and mature with each passing morning. If you talk to Him, He will talk to you. He will teach you how to understand His inspirations. One day you will be inspired to do something for Him, and whatever it is will make you feel good about yourself that day. It is a lot easier than you think. Attend the services offered by your religion. If you have no religion, then pick one. Pray. It will eventually work miracles.

Fifth, and finally, *there are family and friends of yours that have passed away who are in a favorable place with God. They are watching out for you. They may even be the vehicle that God will use to inspire you.* I was very close to my dad. Since he died in 2008 I have spoken to him through prayer, but for much of that time, I was disappointed that he never made himself known to me. He never seemed to be listening. I wondered if he cared; maybe he was mad at me for some reason. I didn't know, but I was discouraged. After all that time we spent together in the stores and all the lessons that I learned from him, I thought we had a special relationship. I began to believe that I was wrong.

Dad was a heavy smoker for many years and suffered from emphysema. He also contracted lung cancer. After an aggressive surgery, he recovered and lived ten years cancer free. There was no such surgical cure for his emphysema, which is a slow and tortuous way to die. His disease progressed over a couple of decades, but the last year of his life was particularly difficult. He spent his last two months or so in an inpatient hospice facility. That was tough on my dad, but it was also tough on my mom, me and my three siblings and his grandchildren, brothers and sisters. We all visited and spent time with him often. My mom was there every day.

One Sunday, my brother Michael was visiting Dad. Dad was near the end, and Michael needed some inspiration. He walked down the hall and found a Bible. He flipped the Bible open and found himself in the Gospel according to Matthew, chapter 6, verses 25–34. In part, it reads:

> I warn you, then: don't worry about your livelihood, what you are to eat, or drink, or use for clothing. Is not your life more than food? Is not the body more valuable than clothes? Look at the birds in the sky. They do not sew or reap, they gather nothing into barns; yet your heavenly father feeds them. Are not you more important than they? Enough, then, of worrying about tomorrow. Let tomorrow take care of itself. Today had trouble enough of its own.

Michael was comforted by the passage as it was so representative of how my dad lived his life, and the advice he gave to us: do the right thing today, and worry about tomorrow when it gets here. Michael was so moved by the passage that when Dad passed a short time later, he convinced us all that we should put it on Dad's prayer card. We did, and Michael wrote a moving eulogy about my dad and the lessons that were now forever on the back of his prayer card. I keep that prayer card on my nightstand, and from time to time I take a moment to read it and remind myself of the special way that Dad lived his life.

That was February 2008. I was diagnosed in July 2012, and in October of that same year I went for the inpatient treatment that was so integral to the miracle-inspired decision I described in chapter 10. That treatment was extremely difficult to endure, and April was at my bedside every single day, enduring that treatment with me as personally as if she was receiving the treatment herself. Faye was the nurse that cared for me on most of the day shifts. Faye was very attentive, and we got to know each other as the days passed. She knew I worked in healthcare, and she knew I was Catholic. We had these things in common, so she, April, and I talked frequently. I never told her about my dad or the verses that were on the back of his prayer card. I had no reason to, and I did not bring the prayer card with me to the hospital. It never left my nightstand.

One of the mornings during my treatment, Faye came into my room where April and I were settling in for another long day. She was startled. She looked uncomfortable. She was not her normal self. She looked at April and I; she stuttered and hesitated as she spoke. "I don't know why I am telling you this…I could get fired for even bringing this up…but I have to tell you something…I don't know why…but I just have to tell you." She went on, "Look at the birds in the sky…God takes care of them. Think of how much He must love you." I thought this was a little odd, but I did not make the connection at first. I guess I was out of it with all of the drugs that were running through my veins, but April was stunned. It was the message from the back of Dad's prayer card.

April explained to both me and Faye that she was praying to my dad on her way to the hospital that morning. She was distressed at the toll that the treatments were taking on me. In her prayers that morning, she asked my dad to please be with me in the hospital. She implored my dad to give us a sign, anything to let us know that he was with us, that he was with me during this difficult treatment. Faye then gave me a book; it was a little book of daily prayers. Again, she didn't know why, but she felt that she had to give it to me. That prayer book sits on my nightstand right next to my dad's prayer card to this day.

You have family and friends in heaven too. They are watching over you. You may never get a sign from them, but they are there. My dad responded to April's prayers that day. I now know that he is watching over me.

So now you know my story. I have shared with you all that I can remember to help you understand and hopefully come to believe that miracles happen every day. They happen to all of us. They have happened in the past, and they will happen again in the future. When we recognize them, they build our trust, and they ignite our hope. Have you never experienced a miracle? I bet you have. Think about it. Look a little harder. Open your mind to the possibility. Say a prayer every day. If you haven't recognized a miracle yet, you will sometime in the future.

Be patient. You will soon come to recognize your own miracle-inspired decisions.

ABOUT THE AUTHOR

Frank Danza is a Senior Vice President at Northwell Health, one of the nation's largest private healthcare systems headquartered in Long Island, New York. During his fourteen years at Northwell Health, Frank has assumed various strategic and executive responsibilities in finance, revenue cycle, and hospital operations. Prior to joining Northwell Health in 2004, Frank was a partner at the accounting and consulting firm Arthur Andersen, where he successfully consulted to the health insurance and hospital industries. He and his wife, April, were born and continued to reside in Brooklyn, New York, where they raised their two daughters, Christina and Madeline. Frank is a certified public accountant and an active member in his community, having served as a trustee and finance committee member at his Catholic parish and treasurer at his Catholic grade school academy. Frank can be reached at fdanzanotalone@gmail.com.

CPSIA information can be obtained
at www.ICGtesting.com
Printed in the USA
BVHW030257070220
571592BV00002B/9

9 781644 929650